hungry for wine

SEEING THE WORLD THROUGH THE LENS OF A WINE GLASS

CATHY HUYGHE

PROVISIONS PRESS

2015

Photos, Cathy Huyghe.

Cover design, Laurie Rosenthal Seiler.

Editor, Becky Sue Epstein.

Published by Provisions Press
www.ProvisionsPress.com

Citation:
Cathy Huyghe. Hungry for Wine. Provisions Press, 2015.

ISBN: 978-1-944159-20-7 (Print Version)
eISBN: 978-1-944159-21-4 (ebook Version)

Table of Contents

Dedications

For Mom and Dad, who gave me the very best start, who showed me how to work and how to love.

For Ethan and Leo:

This book represents much of what I did while I was traveling away from home. To sacrifice even a few hours, much less days and days, of witnessing and encouraging your growth was mighty motivation to make these essays worth my time away from you. But sometimes, to put it simply, a writer must write. I hope and pray that in your lives you also find the work that you believe you were meant to do on this Earth.

For Buster, My Love:

Your affection and utterly unwavering encouragement has been, countless times, like a gush of support that blows like the very luckiest wind at my back. You have somehow figured out how to provide kangaroo care, even for my sometimes tumultuous mind, from thousands of miles away.

You are my blessing in this world, and I love you. Ferociously.

(As you know.)

A bucket of Sangiovese grapes that will go into a Brunello di Montalcino wine.

Introduction

Some people see the world in a grain of sand. I see it in a glass of wine.

My relationship to wine – my hunger for it – started out simply enough.

Back in 2007 I started drinking wine because it just tasted *good*. I liked that I felt *good* when I drank a glass or two. And I especially liked how people opened up when we drank it together.

That, I have come to see, was the hook: wine helped me get to know people.

People like my friends, who I wanted to know better. People like new friends, who I wanted to include in my circle of relationships. And totally unknown people in far off places too, people I imagined had a *way* to their lives that somehow included the simple, uncomplicated pleasure of wine.

These were the people I wanted in my life. So I set out to invite them there, in the way I knew how.

By writing.

Back in 2007 I committed to drinking wine, and writing about it, every day for 365 days. That became the name of my first-ever blog: 365daysofwine.com.

(Tough assignment, right?)

I was living in Boston at the time, so drinking wine every day was a way for me to orient myself – to wine as a new subject but even moreso to the city of Boston, as a fully-fledged adult now, rather than the carefree graduate student I was when I moved there the first time a few years earlier.

It wasn't as though "365" – as I came to call the blog, very affectionately – took up all of my time. It couldn't have. I was working at the time for a project on the Middle East, based at Harvard Law School's Program on Negotiation, and I was a first-time parent of twin boys who were, at that point, less than two years old.

I joke that raising twins drove me to drink... Except it wasn't for the reasons you'd think.

Having twins did not make my life crazy and out of control. Quite the opposite, in fact: the kids were FUN (twins in particular are a walking comedy routine), keeping them on a schedule did amazing things for my own schedule, and best of all my husband proved himself to be the most competent and imaginative co-parent I could have ever hoped for.

It was a very creative, very resourceful time in my life.

So no, having twins did not drive me to drink.

Having twins did, however, completely change my relationship to time, and *that* is what opened the window to writing about wine.

That's because I started to think in 20-minute increments.

Before kids, if I had 20 minutes of free time, I would read the newspaper or have a cup of tea or browse through a magazine. Very casual and no-rush about it.

Now, if I had 20 minutes before the kids woke from a nap, say, I'd think to myself, "Twenty minutes! You have 20 minutes! Do you know what you could do in *20 minutes*?!"

What I could do in 20 minutes was make serious headway into a blog post. More and more, those blog posts wanted to be about wine.

The other part of my life at that point was dedicated to the project in the Middle East. I remember visiting Sanliurfa, in southeastern Turkey, with my co-workers and talking with them about 365.

"Nice idea," they said.

"Wish I had the time to do that," they said.

"What an unusual project," they said, "especially since you're here and, well, wine is... not. What do you do on the days you have to miss?"

Sanliurfa is not a place where alcohol flowed freely, I remember writing on the blog. Instead, music served as a social lubricant, replacing alcohol in that corner of the world to relax tensions. Those were the few days that year that I skipped tasting and writing about wine and wrote instead about substitutes for wine that also enabled me to get to know people better.

I didn't know it then, but that trip to Turkey planted the seeds for three recurrent themes that would develop later in my work: the unique role that alcohol plays (and does not play) in Muslim-influenced societies, an acute interest in wines produced in areas of conflict, and non-traditional forms of diplomacy.

In this book you'll see those themes emerge, among several others – in the chapter on the "hero wine" of Turkey and how wine brands market wine when it's forbidden to market wine; and in the chapter on wine from Syria and Lebanon that's produced despite the war at the winery's doorstep.

But those stories were still several years away, and I wasn't yet prepared in either my wine knowledge or my experience to write them.

First there was 365, and Boston, and the baby steps I needed to take, in order to find my voice and my feet in the world of writing about wine.

———

Writing about wine every day in a place like Boston gives you the lay of the land like no other. Which streets are deserts and which are oases of taste. Which shops have the friendliest staff. When the tastings happen, and where the most unusual bottles are opened.

I began to see the city, and its people, through the lens of a wine glass.

Drinking wine every day wasn't hard. It was a lot like learning a new word – once you learn it, you start seeing it *everywhere*. It turns out that Boston's wine scene was also *everywhere*. It was in the obvious places, of course, like tastings at wine shops and dinners at restaurants. But what was often more compelling was when wine spilled over those expected scenarios, the way a movie shoot on a stage set sometimes spills over into the street. I began "finding" wine that good friends had tucked away years and years ago in the basements of their homes; I found it being taught at community centers; I found it at a garage sale on Cape Ann, north of Boston; on a quiet night in Brookline I even found a very special bottle – a 1973 Gaja Sperss from Barolo – that my host had forgotten he had.

Wine opened the door to all of these places, and it opened the path to getting to know people better.

So sip by sip, my interest deepened. Not my knowledge, necessarily – it would be a few months before I enrolled in actual coursework about tasting and analyzing wine. But I was laying the foundation with interest, layer upon layer of it, and lots of questions.

They were the same questions, I see now, that every new wine drinker has at first but is often too shy (or too intimidated) to ask.

Why *does* this white wine smell like flowers, and that one like gasoline?

Why does this red wine from California cost so much more than that white wine from Italy?

Why is the label on this bottle so abstract, while the label on that bottle looks very recognizably like a French château?

Why are people being so specific about which glass to use?

I thought that I could smell some of the things people say they can smell, like cherries and tobacco. But green apple versus yellow apple? And lychee? What is lychee, anyway?

My interests and the questions started to develop a pattern, and a few months into the 365daysofwine project, I had discovered two things.

First, that I found the narrative of a wine – the prose of it, so to speak – more compelling than an analytical tasting note or a bullet-pointed list of descriptors. It's a preference that shapes my writing to this day, and it influences how I try to engage readers: not everyone loves to read about specific aromas or flavors, but everyone loves a story.

And second, that tasting wine was a lot more fun, and a lot less intimidating, when I did it with a friend.

So that's what I did as often as possible – attended tastings with a friend or two – and, when I went alone, I imagined that that friend was with me. The readership of the blog began to grow and other people volunteered to write for it (more and more people to know through wine!), and I incorporated this "imaginary friend" component into the 365daysofwine style guide.

Imagine you're standing outside an event, I encouraged the authors. Loop your arm through theirs and say, "We're going to go in there together, and taste some wine, and talk to people, and have fun. If we learn something about wine along the way, all the better."

That's key, it turns out, when you're learning something new. You "wade in" with what you already know – your friend, say, or your uncanny ability to pick *just the right person* to strike up a conversation with. You're on firm ground and feeling confident. Then, a dose at a time, you add new layers of information and experience. Slowly and incrementally, your knowledge and your confidence expands.

It was this ground-level approach of 365daysofwine that clicked with readers, I think, exactly because it was approachable and friendly. And the relaxed environment we created and communicated was, it turns out, ideal for learning about wine, little by little and sip by sip.

———

The other thing that came through in the writing back then – that I hope still comes through in my writing now – was *curiosity*. I was, and am, endlessly curious about wine and about what it takes to bring a bottle of wine to the table.

My hunger for wine is driven by this boundless curiosity.

So it's easy to answer the question I'm asked most often about how I'm able to do something so appealing (taste wine and travel and write about it) on such a regular or even a daily basis. What sustains that level of interest?

It's a question that, more and more, I turn around to the asker: imagine what would happen if you picked one thing, one thing you really (really) love, and you allowed that to be your prism? What if that one thing was the lens you used to see the whole world? What if that one thing was your kaleidoscope, and your perception of the world changed every time you made a half-turn?

That one thing you really love changes with each person, of course. People have answered with everything from photography to the weather to cultural adaptations of the potato. (Not kidding.)

For me, with 365daysofwine, wine was doing exactly what I'd hoped it would do: helping me get to know people better. The circle of friends I came to know through wine grew, and grew some more. People subscribed to the blog and the newsletter. More people came to the events we wrote about. And the blog itself got good reviews.

It was flattering, of course, and the reviews were helping me to move toward my second goal of starting the blog, which was to establish myself as a wine writer. Then as now, paid staff positions as journalists were transparently thin on the ground, so I saw the blog as a platform and a launch pad to "real" (read "paid") assignments.

That took a while. So in the meantime, I saw an opportunity to develop my love (my hunger) for wine and wine writing into a business enterprise.

It was called Red White Boston which, as the description in our Executive Summary said, makes it easy to drink wine, learn about wine, and love wine in the Boston area. Very short, sassy, daily emails alerted subscribers to exclusive offers and of-the-moment local wine events. They delivered a quick jolt of interest and information. Each email ended with a "call to action," namely the what-where-when, the cost, and how the reader could participate in each program.

The network grew. My exposure to the *people* of wine grew even more. And I started to learn how the business of wine worked, something that would come in very handy later.

In October 2010, we launched our very own iPhone app, a location-based service full of 30-second videos about recommended wines available at our network of partner retail wine shops throughout Boston.

We also launched the Red White Tasting Crew, which was a selected group of social media influencers who came together monthly to meet a featured producer, taste their wines, and generate online buzz about them. It was relaxed and fun – an extension, really, of the tone we set with 365daysofwine.

My biggest takeaway from these events was understanding that, no matter how robust a social media presence we had, nothing beats face-to-face interaction, especially not when it comes to wine.

Events were the part of the Red White Boston model where it all came together, "it all" being the people and the place and the wine and the food. Eating and drinking is something we do every day and, fortunately, sometimes that everyday experience reaches the exceptional level.

———

Eventually, a few years later, I moved away from Boston and away from the Red White Boston business model. Life has a way of leading us to new places, even though we didn't really think we wanted to leave the old place behind.

Life landed me in Atlanta. Red White Boston was in the rear view mirror but the lessons learned from the business sat on the passenger seat next to me, like a co-navigator offering directions for the road ahead.

I started to see the next phase of my wine life emerge on the horizon. I knew it would involve writing – always in my life, I think, there will be writing. And that writing would now be about the business and the politics of the wine industry. Before I left Boston, I'd finished my journalism degree at Harvard. So I knew about pitching articles and the mechanics of building a portfolio. Slowly my "clip folder" grew.

Writing a story about wine is, for me, like trimming a tree branch: you either uncover another one underneath it, or else a new story grows out stronger and richer than the one before. Once I'd decided that my "swim lane" would be the business of wine, a whole forest of story ideas grew and emerged.

I set my sights on writing for Forbes.com, which meant writing the kind of articles I'd write as if I were already a columnist for them. So I wrote, for example, about buying a vineyard for *Worth* magazine. I traveled to Beirut and wrote about making wine in a war zone for *The Atlantic*, the BBC, *Decanter*, and DailyBeast.com.

This was all part of the vetting process to write for Forbes.com. And it worked. Wine became, for me, even more of an access point than it was before. I began this journey of wine in order to get to know people better. Which I did, in spades. Now I was shifting gears to get to know people better not just in Boston but everywhere. And I've come to extrapolate the lessons I'd learned in Boston to the broader, global context.

For almost ten years, wine has been my conversation-starter. Now in my writing, wine is my medium of choice to better understand people, cultures, politics, business, motivations, and passions. Wine has become a big part of how I communicate, and what I communicate about, whether it's the Greek economy or politics in the Middle East or entrepreneurs in Portland, Oregon. Wine has helped me understand the interplay of passion and business, and the mystery that holds them in balance.

Seeing the world through a glass of wine, indeed.

The advantage of writing online is the data and the analytics generated by the "hits" of people clicking through to the articles. I could study what it is about wine (and my articles about wine) that draws people in, that makes them read more, that makes them come back for my next post and the one after that. Most often, it isn't the wine per se or the technical evaluation of it or the "tasting notes."

What draws us in are the bridges, and the stories. What draws us in are the narratives around more common-ground topics like politics, entrepreneurship, technology, and the simple question of what wine to drink with dinner – things my readers are already interested in, and are already comfortable with – that are given a new dimension, when seen through the lens of a glass of wine.

Everyone may not understand wine, but everyone does understand passion.

Passionate people are the ones who are Hungry for Wine, and these are the people that I find and whose stories I tell.

————

There's a trajectory to the stories collected in this book about how to see the world through the lens of a wine glass. It's organized into twelve chapters, and each chapter is focused on one bottle of wine and its particular refraction of light, so to speak, through that lens.

The first chapter looks at how to live your wine life with no regrets. It's about what happens when you reach the end of your life and you realize that all of the "special occasions" you've been waiting for – all of the times you could have opened that special bottle – have actually passed you by.

The second chapter is about the early stages of falling in love with wine; it's an excerpt from 365daysofwine.com, about a wine and poetry event in Cambridge, Massachusetts. Then in the third chapter we move onto Portland, Oregon to meet people who not only fell in love with wine but built their lives around it as entrepreneurs and winemakers. They are also community leaders for another generation of up-and-coming winemakers.

In Chapter Four we move from one kind of hunger to another, from emotional hunger to physical hunger. We meet people in vineyards around the world who rely on their jobs as migrant workers to actually put food on the table for their families.

By this point I had turned a corner in my own hunger for wine, and began traveling internationally to write about it. One of the farthest reaches I've traveled was to Patagonia and Chile, literally to the end of the Earth. What I found, as I describe in Chapter Five, was a country in a challenging and creative state of flux, in its winemaking too, especially as it reaches out across the Pacific for new markets.

In Chapter Six we look at another wine producing country in transition, this time driven by the domestic turmoil of a financial crisis. In Greece, the crisis has interesting repercussions for the wine industry: new university graduates who grew up on family farms and vineyards dreamed instead of an urban life, with college degrees and office jobs in the city. But, because of the crisis, job opportunities became minimal to non-existent, so they now find themselves returning to the vineyards.

Turkey is experiencing another kind of crisis, this one more political and religious in nature as it relates to the wine industry there. In Chapter Seven we look at what's called a "hero wine" because a journalist in Istanbul simply wrote about it; by writing about it he also defied government regulations against the "promotion" of alcohol, a risk of his job, a fine, and the potential shut-down of his newspaper.

In Chapter Eight we go even deeper into wine as emblematic of political struggle and domestic turmoil. We look at Château Bargylus which is, still, the only modern winery in Syria and it is, still, producing its signature white and red wines despite war conditions throughout the country. This is a brave wine, made by brave people, who are dedicated to the idea that Syria is about more than religion and more than its regime.

Chapter Nine looks to northeastern Italy for a historical look at war and the establishment of vineyards. Some people in the region of Friuli have lived in the same place their whole lives yet, because of the flow of history and wars in the twentieth century, that place has been part of three different countries in their single lifetime. Livio Felluga's story is of one person's search for a territory during that tumultuous century. He found his own territory anchored by the terroir of the vineyards.

Rioja's history is similarly rich and complex though in different ways. In Chapter Ten we look at how Rioja has developed as a winemaking region, and how its history and the passage of time influences its wines. We visit an underground "cemetery" where wines age for years and sometimes decades, maturing as they go and developing the personality that has come to define this region.

If Rioja is rooted in its history, then South Africa is betting on its future. In Chapter Eleven we explore how a winery near Cape Town is forging a new identity of hospitality for its workers, as they break decisively away from the apartheid system whose echoes still reverberate. In some ways the business culture of South Africa is still a question of survival of the fittest, one winery owner explained, but her way forward bucks that mentality.

In Chapter Twelve we meet some of the original faces of Hungry for Wine, which was initially a film project I created a few years ago, when a colleague (who's a videographer) and I went to Napa to interview on camera several winemakers I knew who seemed, truly, hungry for wine. Chapter Twelve considers their perspectives on lives lived as Hungry for Wine.

Quite a lot of tasting was involved as I did the legwork for those twelve chapters. Tasting, and thinking, and tasting some more and thinking about what I was tasting. At one point, close to the end of writing this book, I suddenly felt like I was losing sight of the reason I started drinking wine in the first place: because it tasted good, and I felt good when I drank it, especially with friends. Suddenly, though, it didn't seem possible anymore to *just drink* without overthinking. In the Conclusion I describe how I returned – quickly, and with gusto – to the simple pleasure of the wine that's in my glass.

——

As a wine writer today, my point of view is often angled toward economics, politics, and the spirit of entrepreneurship, as well as the passion, innovation, and creativity that go along with it. That's why you'll see these themes reverberate throughout these chapters.

The spirit of Hungry for Wine is pulsing all around the world today, from Prague to Cape Town, from Lebanon to France, from Napa to Bordeaux. And it isn't letting up anytime soon. That's why there will be other *Hungry for Wine* books. *Hungry for Wine: Italy*, say. *Hungry for Wine: China. Hungry for Wine: California.* And so on.

But this book, or any book after it, is not meant to be an exhaustive study or educational effort about wine. It is not meant to tell you "everything you need to know" about wine.

It's meant to whet your appetite for it, by showing wine in the context of the everyday lives of real people. It's meant, above all, to make wine *relatable*.

I earnestly hope that you'll enjoy the journey of this book. And I especially hope that you'll find yourself even more Hungry for Wine.

Hungry for Wine Manifesto

I believe that the people of wine matter most.

I believe there is room for eye-to-eye contact over a glass of wine.

I believe that wine does much more than quench thirst. I believe it satisfies a hunger – for community, connection, friendship, understanding, and also a pleasurable, companionable buzz.

I believe that there are people who love wine and want to know, sincerely, the story of where it comes from.

I believe in the value of knowing what it took to bring a bottle of wine to your table.

I believe in the value of a humane, contextualized "experience note" for wine tasting.

I believe there is room for the smart, savvy use of technology to enhance the experience of wine, and to lessen the struggle of the people who make and sell it.

I believe in building bridges to wine, in engaging people in a topic that's familiar to them – technology, say, or entrepreneurialism, or a love for food or travel – and using it as a bridge to enjoying wine.

I believe that there are people who won't relate to the wine necessarily but who will relate to the story of the people behind it – of the career-changers, say, or the city kid who goes off to work in a vineyard, or the couple in a village in Italy who make just enough wine to satisfy the guests in their small restaurant.

Hungry for Wine is my bet that there's room for all of that.

It is also my promise to find them and shine the light on these people who are hungry.

For wine.

One small storage shed breaks the steep slope of the landscape of the Douro Valley of Portugal.

Chapter One
How to Live Your Wine Life with No Regrets

An elderly friend of mine – I call him The Young Man – treads like a mountain goat down the creaky stairs of his home in West Cambridge, Massachusetts. It is a hot summer evening but, as we descend into his cellar, the temperature of the air cools appreciably and we both feel a sense of subterranean relief.

A psychiatrist by training, and a long-time faculty member at Harvard Medical School, The Young Man has lived in this house for more than fifty years. He knows every crevice and fault and advantage but, at age 93, he steps gingerly down.

He moves slowly toward the wine cellar in the basement, one deliberate step at a time. I follow. I could see the wet splotches on the back of his short-sleeve, collared shirt where drops of his perspiration had soaked through.

"There really isn't that much to see," he says to me over his narrow, frail shoulder.

He doesn't see me roll my eyes as he takes one step, and then another.

He'd told me before about a bottle of Grand Armagnac he'd bought decades ago because it dated from the year of his birth, 1914. I could see his eyes brighten, even behind the thickness of his bifocal glasses, with the excitement and the resonance of such a purchase and such a wine.

If this was any indication of what he had tucked away, his protests about "not much to see" were charmingly self-effacing.

But by the time I leave his home that night, I realize that – aside from the Armagnac and one or two other bottles – he is right. There really is not much to see. I am disappointed, but not because I'd lost my chance to uncover a treasure trove of vintage wines.

I am disappointed because so many lovely wines he had stored away were well past their prime and almost undrinkable. They'd wasted away in their bottles down in that cellar, behind lock and key. As though they were living beings, buried alive, secured away from the pleasure they could have brought. Echoes of Poe's "The Cask of Amontillado" throb in my head.

"I've been saving these bottles for a special occasion," my friend had said as he searched for something on a low shelf in his wine cellar, which is really a locked closet around the corner from dusty storage boxes that hadn't been opened for untold decades. "But all the special occasions seem to have passed me by."

My friend points to an eight-bottle rack in the left-hand corner of the uppermost shelf in his cellar. He tells me about a Frenchwoman named Françoise who shuttled the once-valuable wines into his possession. He remembers every bottle's provenance, but he never opened a single one of them.

It is clear, as I listen to him talk, that it was more about Françoise's attention, and her pleasure in bringing him the wines, than it was about following through to open and actually drink them.

He has watched from the sidelines as the wines approached their prime, peaked, then slid downhill. So there the bottles sit as we find them that summer evening: unsavored, unappreciated, and clouded by regret.

———

Years ago, when Dorothy Gaiter and John Brecher were wine columnists at the *Wall Street Journal*, they initiated the annual Open That Bottle Night (OTBN) to prevent exactly those kinds of regrets. OTBN is a designated occasion when fine wines and wines attached to fine memories are consumed. By designating that one night, we're given the prompt of an occasion, as so many of us attach some kind of permission to the opening of a special bottle.

Normally OTBN passes by me without incident, because I simply don't have any bottles that are too special to open.

Don't misunderstand – I have special bottles, many of them (thankfully). One of the earliest was an Oregon Pinot Noir from Patricia Green. When I brought it home I literally marked the date on my calendar – two years ahead of that night – when I planned to open it.

And I did.

Because what I'm after here is to be a wine *consumer*, not a wine collector.

What I'm after is a willingness to open special bottles just because. Just because it's Tuesday. Or just because a friend has come around. Or just because I'm enjoying an evening of solitude. Or just because – or especially because – on bad days too, we can always find things to be grateful for, and things to toast.

What I'm after, in other words, is to live my wine life with no regrets.

———

Back in his cellar that summer night, The Young Man's hands shake, but only a little, as he pulls out a bottle of 1970 Château Rauzan-Gassies from Margaux. He tilts his head of cloud-white hair thoughtfully to one side.

He pauses.

Then he slides the bottle back in its place.

We step out of the closet, he locks it again behind us, and we make our way slowly back up the stairs, one step, and then another.

I look down at my feet. This night wasn't meant to be one of those special occasions he had been waiting for.

No night was.

It made me sad.

It wasn't only about waiting for a special occasion. It was also about a generosity of spirit, and a willingness to *create* a special occasion rather than wait for one to come to you.

Maybe there's a correlation between being hungry for wine and being willing to create the circumstances to enjoy it.

—

As I wrote this chapter, I knew that I'd want to track down an old bottle of Château Rauzan-Gassies, the wine my friend had pulled from his rack and then, after a pause, slid it back in.

Rauzan-Gassies is a Bordeaux property identified as one of fifteen Second Growth properties in the 1855 classification. The 70-acre Margaux estate dates back to the sixteenth century, and today its wines are made primarily from Cabernet Sauvignon followed by Merlot, Petit Verdot, and Cabernet Franc.

It took a few tries to find a wine that old. My friend's was from 1970, but I'd be happy to get somewhere in the ballpark.

First we tried online, and succeeded in finding a single bottle from 1982. That historical vintage in Bordeaux has won wide and critical acclaim for its red wines, but the success in Margaux specifically (where this property is located) was inconsistent. Expectations were mixed at best. Plus it was expensive, it would have to be shipped from England, and delivery costs alone would triple the pricetag.

Hmm.

I decided to keep trying.

Next I called my friend Doug, who is a Bordeaux specialist and runs a set of retail wine shops in Atlanta, where I live.

A bottle from 1970 will be hard to find, he said, but he offered an alternative from the same vintage from another Bordeaux estate: 1970 Château Talbot in a magnum. He could personally vouch for its authenticity directly from the source; counterfeit bottles of Bordeaux have become an unfortunate problem worldwide, and it's wise to be on alert. And magnums – double the size of a regular bottle – are an advantageous format for holding aged wines.

We were having dinner with a group of friends the following night – a celebratory birthday dinner – so with the no-regrets sentiment fresh in mind, we brought the bottle with us, opened and decanted it, and toasted everyone at the table who has managed to live more years than the wine itself.

The 1970 Château Talbot was lovely, of course. It was a little short on the finish, but otherwise mellow, with red fruits that echoed more than they sang, tobacco notes that lingered more than they intruded, and spice notes of cinnamon and cocoa that were more slow-burn that hot-flash.

In the meantime, a friend of mine in Italy managed to find three (three!) bottles of the 1970 Château Rauzan-Gassies. They were in Belgium but so, it turned out, would we be: my husband grew up in a town on the coast of Belgium, and we were making a surprise visit in a few weeks with the kids to celebrate his parents' 50th wedding anniversary. We secured the wine, left one bottle with my husband's family, and carried the other two home with us on the flight. We gave it some time to settle, and looked forward to opening it as soon as possible after that.

Tasting Note: 1970 Château Rauzan-Gassies

That opportunity presented itself just a few weeks later. I'd have gladly opened a bottle simply because it was a random Wednesday evening, but some friends who we knew to be lovers of Bordeaux invited us for dinner. The "special occasion" was simply that we'd open these bottles and share them with people we knew would also be interested in how the wine tastes after all these years.

It didn't start out well. I removed the foil from one of the bottles and immediately saw that the cork was damaged and moldy. Not a good sign. I tried, very gently, to remove it with a corkscrew but it crumbled to bits when I pulled, so much so that the corkscrew came back out of the bottle without the cork. It had almost completely disintegrated.

19

We struggled with it, and after some time (and some mess) we managed to pour a few small tastes and passed them around. It was awful, as we sadly anticipated. Vinegary. Oxidized. No fruit. And way too much funk.

But! We had a second bottle! What are the chances of having *two* faulty wines from the same source?

Pretty high, apparently. The second bottle followed exactly the same pattern as the first. Damage and mold under the foil. Crumbly cork. Oxidized wine inside.

Ugh.

It was disappointing, to say the least. Disappointing, that is, that the wine in its prime had never been drunk. Disappointing, too, that whoever held onto this wine for so long had never opened or enjoyed it. I was sad the way I was sad for my friend, The Young Man, as we walked back up the stairs from his cellar that night. No night and no special occasion was special *enough*.

It's like not being *hungry enough* for wine, and living with the regret of that.

That wasn't the (wine) life I wanted. What I wanted was a life of interest, of bottles opened, of special occasions enjoyed, of regular occasions honored too.

This doesn't mean that life is one big party. Hunger ebbs and flows, naturally. And there are different ways and different reasons to open a bottle of wine, at different times. You can open a bottle of wine with gusto, as you describe enthusiastically and dramatically your latest weekend adventure. You can open it with a fun flourish, to entertain your audience. You can open it quietly, as you commiserate with a friend who's sitting at your kitchen counter, sharing their troubles.

You can also open a wine too late. Which is what I hope to avoid.

The red boots of a harvest worker peek out from the tall vines in the Prosecco region of northern Italy.

Chapter Two
How to Find Your Feet – and Your Voice – in Wine

As I drank and wrote about wine every day, for 365 days, the city of Boston itself became a character in my writing. I started to find the What and the When, and also the Where and the Why, of the most interesting bottles. The contours of the city started taking shape, while the week also started to find its rhythm.

On Monday at noon it may have been a refreshing Sauvignon Blanc on a terrace overlooking the Boston Common. On Tuesday for dinner maybe it was ragu and Barbera – or steamed Wellfleet littlenecks and Vermentino – in the historically Italian neighborhood of the North End. Wednesday's after-work ritual may have been the tiny tasting room tucked below State Street. On Thursday it was dinner at home or with friends who arrived with the latest recommendation from the Newbury Street wine shop nestled under their arm.

Friday, to start the weekend, it could have been game night or the theater with a pre-show glass or two in Bay Village. Saturday may have meant shopping in the South End with a quick lunch and by-the-glass on Tremont Street. Sunday was sometimes dim sum and Riesling in Chinatown, or a trip a few miles out to Southborough for the latest case allotment from Burgundy, or to the world's wine-friendliest beer place in Concord, or for an exceptionally good value wine in Andover.

I discovered that Boston is a treasure trove of great wines and their stories, and slowly I started to learn where and how to find them. Because when it comes to enjoying wine, as this first year so clearly demonstrated, what's outside the bottle counts too.

There are plenty of places and times and ways to get your "fix" of wine in Boston. That's a bit of a confession, I suppose, because during that year I became addicted to wine, since I did drink it every day and wrote about it in some fashion at least once every 24 hours.

The good news is that it wasn't the alcohol or the buzz per se that I became addicted to.

It was the *stories* behind the wine.

For me every bottle, every glass, and even every sip has its own story to tell, depending on where it's from and who I'm with when I'm drinking it and what I'm eating alongside it and why I've selected that particular bottle in the first place.

For me, wine was about the *challenge*. Not of knowing more bits of knowledge than someone else. Wine challenges me because it is NEW every single time. No two bottles are the same, no two glasses, no two sips.

It's the same with Boston, which is one of the most uniquely provincial and opinionated cities in America. That's true when you're talking politics or recipes for lobster rolls, and it's true when you're talking about wine.

Every neighborhood, and every wine shop in every neighborhood, has its own personality. Every shop's inventory carries the inflection of its owners but also of its customers. Its customers, most likely, are the couple who live up the street or the young college students on their way to a party or the professionals who walk by every day on their way home from work.

———

Drinking wine every day, somewhere in the Boston area, wasn't hard. Aside from finding it at the usual places like restaurants and shops, there were often evening programs organized around a particular theme, like poetry or politics or food.

But even if it was one of those other themes that pulled me through the door, I ended up staying for the wine. And even if I stayed for the wine, it was still about the *context*. It's a gentle and effective approach, and I learned more each time because there was a world around the glass, so to speak, that I could remember. That "world" meant the program, the people I met there, and the conversations we had, which all helped to solidify the experience of the wine in my mind.

One evening, for example, I went to a poetry slam held at Formaggio Kitchen, West Cambridge's renowned cheese shop that manages to be both well-respected and edgy. The person measuring and wrapping up your cheese is just as likely to articulate the intricacies of Brie de Meaux as they are to wear nose rings and tattoos. That person, I learned at their "Cheese and Poetry" event that night, is also likely to be a lyricist and a romantic.

Poetry, I can do. Cheese also. They were both familiar territory, and the organizers had arranged one poem and one cheese for each of five "flights." The stretch for me was to the wine, which was also added to each flight.

The cheese was mostly from France and Italy. There was also an accompaniment, either a condiment like honey or, in one case, an unusual chestnut flour flatbread sprinkled with salt and sugar. The wines, also mostly from France and Italy, were organic or biodynamic.

And the poets were local, including Simone Beaubien, and James Caroline of Cambridge.

It was James' line, from his poem "Maybe You Didn't Hear Me the 1st Time," that caught my ear first:

I turn every corner like your voice is one block over.

Snap.

At poetry slams, you snap your fingers – instead of clapping – to show your appreciation for a poem and its performer. I was also snapping because the poems set the mood, and I realized I was surrounded by people I wanted to get to know better. Each of them, like me, had been drawn to this program of words and wine. We had carved the time for it out of a cold February night and here we were, shoulder to shoulder and ready to tune in.

———

Formaggio is a small, tight shop with much of its floor space occupied by shelving or cases full of high-quality gourmet products. There is always standing room only, and there's a sense of the Sardinian pasta nudging your elbow or the Corsican olive oil tapping you on the shoulder, volunteering for duty.

The wine selection is small and "tightly curated," which is not a phrase that the staff would necessarily use. They narrow their selection of wines the same way that they narrow their selection of rice or chocolate or jams: they're looking for things that other stores don't have or can't get. (This was before the widespread use of online ordering, when a differentiating factor for a shop was the visibility on their shelves of a unique and limited product.)

Biodynamic wines take pride of place on Formaggio's shelves. Biodynamic producers limit their use of sulfur, which is used to preserve a wine's freshness and shelf life. Formaggio's wine buyer at the time explained that when they select a biodynamic wine, they're looking for a "skillful use" of sulfur. He meant that sulfur would be used as little as possible, even though that increases a wine's volatility and decreases the amount of time it'll last on the shelves.

Biodynamic wines can also be as variable as the weather, and that can be a good thing or a bad thing: bad if you're looking for total consistency from one bottle to another, good if you appreciate the variability inherent in an agricultural product that's produced naturally.

Either way, biodynamic wines take some getting used to. "The wines aren't necessarily consistent," wine buyer David Seaton said, "but the weather isn't consistent either."

That makes sense to me – *snap* – so my tolerance for biodynamic wines and all its variability is fairly high.

Of all the food/cheese/condiment/wine pairings of the evening, the one I enjoyed best was a honey derived from orange and lemon tree nectar (Bottega delle Api Zagara from Campania, Italy) and a wine from the Orvieto DOC by Sergio Mottura in Lazio, Italy. The Orvieto was the only white wine served during the event, and the cheese it was paired with – Ficaccio from Campania, which is made from water buffalo milk – was unusually neutral. So the pairing was reduced, essentially, to the wine and the honey.

Historically, Orvieto was once known for its off-dry style and rich honey flavor though this particular wine was made in a more contemporary style. It was a complementary opposite to the honey, both in texture and in flavor: the Orvieto was smooth and dry, while the honey was coarse and sweet since some sugars from the nectar had crystallized.

The pairing was, well, poetic.

Snap.

Tasting Note: 2008 Sergio Mottura Orvieto Secco

This bottle comes from the Lazio region of Italy, closest to Rome. Lazio, frankly, is not well-regarded for its wine production but this wine makes a case for why-not. Sergio Mottura is best known for his use of the Grechetto grape, which comprises 25% of this Orvieto Secco blend.

The rest is 25% Verdello and 50% Procanico, neither of which are headliners of any wine tasting or book I know. But that is part of the point: so many of Italy's native grapes are hyper local and hyper focused, market trends be damned. The varieties on Mottura's estate, including these three, were selected and whittled down over the years according to their quality as well as their resistance to disease and pests – a clear reminder that wine is, above all, an agricultural product that's farmed within sometimes-harsh agricultural realities.

There is history in this glass – the estate dates back to the thirteenth century – and there are also golden highlights to accentuate the pale yellow color. On the nose you'll find fragrant, tropical fruits as well as wild mint and kitchen herbs like thyme and marjoram. Finishes dry.

Seven Secrets for Daily Wine Drinking

1. Taste a little bit, even a sip or two, every day. The more you taste, the easier it becomes because the experience of wine grows increasingly familiar. The key is to start looking for that experience, and to get in the habit.

2. Accept that you can do this on a budget. There is no better time to be a wine consumer. Why? Restaurants and wine shops are vying for your business by offering special deals here, discount offers there, try-before-you-buy options somewhere else.

3. Overcome the feeling of being overwhelmed. Make friends with your local wine merchant. Sign up for wine communities online. There are resources available. Research them, and choose one or two that are suited to your personality.

4. Take advantage of first-hand opportunities. Winemakers and winery representatives spend a large part of their year (and their budget) visiting various markets and meeting consumers face to face. Sign yourself up as one of those faces they meet.

5. Get your feet wet. Literally. Wine-producing vineyards now exist in every state of the US and, thanks to global warming, vineyards are also being planted in what were previously thought to be regions too cold or inaccessible for grape growing. Find a vineyard near you, and plan a visit.

6. Find new friends who are also interested in wine. Link up with a tasting club. Take a class. Start your own BYOB dinner group. Wine is meant to be shared. Plus it's just more fun that way.

7. Wine is a treat. Treat it like one. Whether it's big-scale like a marketing campaign from a major winery, or small-scale like a person-to-person transaction in your tiny local wine shop, the business of wine is at its best when it's making someone's life better. Move beyond your mundane daily concerns.

Kate and Tom Monroe inside the wine bar at their SE Wine Collective in Portland, Oregon.

Chapter Three
How to Live the
"Wine Lifestyle" Anywhere

That tiny shop in Boston, at a poetry slam no less, isn't exactly where I would have expected to find the things I love about wine – most of all, the other people who love wine too, who have an earnest appreciation of it, who want to keep learning more. They've made wine part of their everyday lives. That's what I call living the "wine lifestyle," and it's one of the things I love most about wine.

But that isn't necessarily what some wine marketers and advertisers call the "wine lifestyle."

For them, it's more often about the beautiful vineyards. The generations-old traditions. The picturesque cellars. The incessantly happy, smiling people, both those who make the wine and especially – especially – those who drink it.

They call it "aspirational advertising." And it works like a charm.

Who wouldn't want that life?

To live in a beautiful place surrounded by beautiful people eating beautiful food, and drinking what must be beautiful wine.

Sign me up.

But here's the thing. There's also a flip side or "B Side" that's more about the realities of living a life in wine. It's the less glamorous, but arguably more important part because it grounds all the beautiful-this beautiful-that and makes it believable rather than air-brushed. There are real problems in the wine industry, problems of ego and environment and an ever-encroaching, menacing homogeneity. There are also the logistical operations, behind the scenes, that make wine *work* by actually moving the bottles from the winery to your table.

So the real "wine lifestyle," for me, means taking the good with the bad. It's what makes wine all the more real, and tangible, and human. It's what you can access even outside physical proximity to any winery or vineyard or wine route.

The wine lifestyle, in other words, is *everywhere*. Everywhere, that is, that you care to look.

————

Portland, Oregon is one of those places where wine is tangible. As in, right there, from one street to another. That's because Portland is home to an impressive network of urban wineries.

An urban winery may not be the very first thing that comes to mind when you think of grapes, or wineries, or even vineyards. But a model for it is rooted in the city of Beaune, in Burgundy, France. Beaune is one of the world's most legendary wine towns thanks to the vineyards and sites that surround it, such as Pommard, Volnay, Savigny-les-Beaune, and Aloxe-Corton.

Imagine the town at the center, a town like Beaune or Portland. The vineyards circle it on the outside and, after the grapes are picked at harvest time, they're transported from the periphery to a winery facility at the center of town, where they're crushed and matured into wine.

It has worked this way for centuries in Burgundy. Portland is newer to the wine scene, of course, but a community of wine entrepreneurs there has adopted Beaune's urban winery model as their own. (Both regions also share Pinot Noir and Chardonnay as their signature grapes. In Burgundy those grapes are grown and mandated by law, while in Oregon they were selected voluntarily and they thrive thanks to its microclimate's affinity to the Burgundian model.)

The vineyard sites that circle Portland are too expensive for most new entrepreneurs and winemakers to buy. So they "rent" the land, which for a winemaker means a contract with the owner of the vineyard to buy the fruit that's grown there. At harvest time, just as in Beaune, the fruit is trucked from the outlying vineyards to a winery at the center of the town, where it's made into wine, bottled, and sold.

This is the model that inspired Portland-based entrepreneurs Kate and Tom Monroe. Their urban winery is called the SE Wine Collective and it replicates, at many important touch points along the way, Beaune's model:

- The "home base" in town.

- The relationships with the growers, who produce grapes according to a mutually-agreed upon set of standards, which often includes organic and/or biodynamic directives.

- The storage and aging of the wines.

- The close proximity to communities of consumers, along with easier access to the broader marketplace.

Urban wineries appeal to entrepreneurs without the capital, the generational history, or the land ownership required of the more recognizable (and arguably less efficient) "château model" where a winery building is surrounded by its estate vineyards.

Those wine entrepreneurs have clustered together and made Portland one of the most livable cities of the wine lifestyle.

———

I'm not sure which came first in Portland, the people with the entrepreneurial, wine-tinged spirit or the community that supported it. It goes back a long time, almost 50 years now. Some slid away (or escaped from) California's wine country in search of a different landscape and maybe a different culture or expectations. Others came from vastly different places for vastly different reasons.

Kate Monroe grew up in France, and her husband Tom developed the business plan for an urban winery while completing his MBA at Washington University in St. Louis, Missouri.

At the time, writing the plan was more of an exercise than a blueprint for reality. Then, after some time for Tom to work in the corporate finance world in New York, the couple decided to take advantage of an opportunity to live and work – and learn the trade – in a small vineyard in France.

There, the way of life was more closely aligned with what they envisioned and wanted to pursue back in the US. The wine industry is notorious, Tom told me, for "attracting retired rich guys. But that wasn't how we were looking at it. The urban winery fits how we wanted to get what we wanted to get out of our lives."

What they wanted to get, apparently, is a business that is also a community and a hub, a gathering place for friends and like-minded people, for other entrepreneurs and casual acquaintances who are all drawn to the energy – the energy of a friendly, pull-up-a-seat approach to wine on one hand, and of a dig-in approach to business on the other.

Kate describes it as a business "in front of our crowd and in our neighborhood, where we could bring wine to people in a different way, and produce wine in a different mindset."

One way to think of the SE Wine Collective – that business in front of their crowd and in their neighborhood – is as an "enological incubator." Making wine, and fostering the future of winemaking too, are both part of the Collective's mission. So the Monroes opened the doors to their winery with a cooperative mindset, where a small group of other new winemakers could also make their own wines, following the same model of leasing vineyards or buying grapes on short- or long-term contracts, and using the Monroes' equipment to create the finished product.

There is a significant initial capital investment for new urban wineries. For the Monroes, it was approximately $180,000 to renovate the building, $160,000 for equipment, and $75,000 in operating costs for launch. But that is nowhere near the investment for new wineries or property in other parts of Oregon, in Beaune, or in the Napa Valley.

The next step, just as in Beaune, is to bring the wine to market, to the community of consumers who are, presumably, within close (urban) proximity. The Monroes opened a wine bar for this purpose: to sell wines made within the cooperative, and as another revenue stream.

The wine bar also features what the Monroes call "inspiration wines," that is, other small-production wines from around the world that share the same philosophy of development.

The cooperative also showcases its wines at events held within the winery space – supper clubs, for example, or weddings or fundraisers.

Working with a variety of winemakers, using grapes from a variety of growers, and distributing those wines to a variety of outlets: that's the diversification of what the SE Wine Collective is about, Kate said. "It allows us to take the eggs out of one basket and experiment a little bit."

That diversification also allows them to have a better public sense than a traditional production winery.

Which brings us back to urban planning and the urban winery model.

Fortunately, Portland has a public that is in tune with the wine, the model, and the broader desire to understand their food and where it comes from.

"We're invested in providing that experience to the client," Kate said. "They deserve to know who makes it. They deserve to appreciate it. Our prices are not inexpensive, and they choose our products because they're invested in the story and in the small artisanal production."

Tasting Note: 2013 Division Pinot Noir "Un"

Each chapter in this book tells the story of what it took to bring a particular bottle of wine to your table. For the most part, the story is about the people who made the wine and the circumstances that the wine emerged from.

For the tasting note for this chapter, the story is also about the transitional phase between when the wine left the urban winery and when I purchased it at the store and brought it home. It involves a distribution network, which in the U.S. most often means a "three tier system" – producers are one tier, distributors (usually state-specific) are the second tier, and the retailer or restaurant where the consumer buys the wine comprises the third tier.

Direct To Consumer sales, or DTC, are a separate category, where the producer sells and/or ships directly to the consumer without the middle two tiers of the distributor or retailer/restaurant. Because profit margins are greater when there are fewer hands for the wines to pass through, and fewer companies or organizations take their cut, DTC sales are an optimal arrangement. Not all wineries have access to DTC sales in all states, however, and the vast majority of wines in the U.S. are still sold through the three-tier system.

The SE Wine Collective, through the wine bar next door to the winery and the event space within it, sells a percentage of their wines DTC. And yes, it's lovely and maybe even optimal to taste the wines *in situ*. But sometimes you need social media to help.

When it came time to taste this wine again, after trying it for the first time with Kate and Tom Monroe in their wine bar in Portland, I took to Twitter. Where, in my home city, could I find this wine, I tweeted.

Two answers – and two retail shops – came back as the answer.

The person who answered the phone at one of the shops had never heard of the wine or the producer, and he also never called back as he said he would once he tracked it down, if he ever did. This underscores the tenuousness – the pure chance and small likelihood – of your wine actually making it to the table of someone who wants it and will appreciate it.

I have always envisioned this book as "the story of twelve bottles of wine and what it took to bring those bottles to the table." This bottle, the "Un" Pinot Noir, illustrates that "bringing a bottle to your table" involves a lot more than crushing grapes. It also involves the people who grew the grapes, who crushed the grapes (maybe as part of an enological incubator), who helped it mature into wine.

And, as maybe the last rung on the ladder, the narratives involve the people who delivered it to the market.

Which brings us to the person who answered the phone at the second shop.

She knew immediately and exactly what I was asking for.

"I love this wine," she said. "Such a cool producer."

They *are* cool.

They're making the wine lifestyle work for them.

They aspired to it and – guess what? – it's coming true.

They worked with the grape growers of three different vineyards in order to make this wine. They're the same growers they've been working with since the beginning. For this vintage they also added a new plot that's been farmed biodynamically. The different fruit, from different places and different farmers, was handled differently and separately in the winery.

I won't make a claim that I can parse out the characteristics of that different fruit.

But here is what I know: what's identifiably "Pinot Noir" comes through for me in this wine. The cranberry, the holiday spices, and especially the earthiness that I love. What's identifiably trendy comes through too, that is, the lower alcohol (12.5% ABV, in this case) and the lighter style that is so appealing, so alluring to wine drinkers (young and old, new and experienced) who prefer not to be hit over the head with any measure of fruit bomb.

This wine is a result of the grapes' growing conditions on the one hand, and stylistic choices on the other. They come together in a wine that is a demonstration of a *lifestyle*, well-lived.

Two migrant workers from the island of Vanuatu had just caught this
rabbit when I came upon them in a Matua vineyard of New Zealand.

Chapter Four
How to Catch a Rabbit, and
What that Says about
Who Harvests Your Grapes

There's a lot to be said for living a life with no regrets, as we saw in Chapter One. But it assumes one very basic condition, namely, that you have a *choice* to make.

Living a wine life with no regrets assumes that you have the luxury of choosing whether to open a bottle of wine, or not. It assumes that you have the luxury of access to wine in the first place. It assumes that, if you're able to buy wine, then presumably the food component of the meal is already taken care of.

We should all be so lucky.

In this chapter we take a deliberate look at another definition of the word *hungry*.

So far, and generally speaking, I use "hungry" to mean passion, and desire, and an intrinsic motivation to participate either in the creation of wine or its enjoyment.

It is, as the saying goes, a "first world problem."

Because being "hungry" also means, well... being hungry.

When I think of the people who are literally hungry for wine I think instinctively of the crews of workers I've met, in vineyards around the world and mostly before 7 am, whose job simply pays the bills. Wine satisfies their hunger because it puts food on the table.

This was brought home to me one day as I was walking through vineyards in New Zealand. I came across a couple of guys dressed in shorts and t-shirts and baseball caps.

One of the guys was holding a large rabbit. They had just caught the rabbit, it turns out, and they were taking it home to cook for dinner. The rabbit was still alive, stunned but still quivering.

My first question, naturally, was how do you even *catch* a rabbit?

My second question was, what are these guys doing here in this vineyard?

———

It turns out that they were seasonal workers from Vanuatu (an island off the northeastern coast of Australia, about 1800 miles from New Zealand) and they were part of a well-executed plan to supply wineries in New Zealand with labor during the grape harvest. They also work other agricultural harvests, and end up spending about four months of the year away from home in order to support themselves and their families.

Here, as I stood face to face with the ni-Vanuata islanders and their quivering rabbit, was the answer to a question I try to ask at every property I visit: who harvests your grapes?

My first indication that this question sheds some unusual light on the topic of hunger in the wine world was several years ago, in Boston, during lunch at a restaurant with a winemaker from eastern Italy, across the Adriatic Sea from Croatia.

Given that geographical position, and at that moment in history, this particular winemaker's region was seeing the flow of immigrants and refugees from the Yugoslav wars of the late 1990s and early 2000s.

The winery needed workers, and indigenous labor for viticulture has been on decline for years. Although the immigrants were Muslim, and had little or no experience with wine as an alcoholic beverage, they were nonetheless excellent gardeners.

(It reminded me of a buffalo milk farm I also visited in southern Italy, where many workers were Hindu immigrants from India. They may not have known anything about dairy farming, but because of their religion they honor cows. So they're excellent caregivers to the herd.)

Panta rei, as they say in Italian. Everything flows. The flow of people. The flow of labor. The flow of religion, and politics, and conflict. The flow has landed these immigrants on a vineyard in eastern Italy, where they tend the vines and grow the grapes to make wine they'll probably never drink.

I thought of this example from Italy on the day that I ran into the crew from Vanuatu. It isn't as though the island of Vanuatu is overrun with vineyards or vineyard workers, either, and it isn't as though Vanuatu has a long and distinguished history as prime grape growing real estate.

But they do have a labor force that's willing to travel for months at a time, and they're welcome in New Zealand. Which is why I crossed paths with that small group of workers in the vineyard. Catching rabbits wasn't officially part of their job, but they were certainly welcome to do that too.

Because rabbits in vineyards are a nuisance from one point of view, while from another view they are protein, nourishment, and a full meal.

———

Sometimes you take a walk in a vineyard, and you're surprised by what you see.

And sometimes you are surprised by who you meet.

Who I've met – the people who physically prune the vines, harvest the grapes, and generally maintain the vineyards – are more answers to my persistent question about the labor of wine.

Who harvests your grapes?

It seems like a simple enough question.

But the answers sketch an interesting and complex profile of shifting demographics in locations all over the world, from migrant labor to organized unions, from full-time staff to the temporarily (or marginally) employed.

In Champagne, for example, the grapes may be picked by a crew of some 200 seasonal workers who travel from Portugal to work the harvest. The crew is organized by one very savvy entrepreneur who himself migrated to France as an agricultural laborer.

In Lebanon, the grapes may be harvested by nomads who set up their camps alongside the roads running through the Bekaa Valley.

In the Douro Valley of Portugal, it may be a crew of workers – both women and men, both older and younger – with a penchant for *fado*. It was pruning season when I visited the Douro Valley, a region where the landscape slopes as much as 65 degrees and, since the use of machinery in the vineyards is nearly impossible, pruning is especially difficult and labor-intensive.

The crew spread themselves through the rows of vines but within close proximity to each other, within earshot. I was driving through the vineyards in a four-wheel drive vehicle – to give you a sense of the terrain – and hopped out so that I could take a picture of these people working in such a dramatic landscape.

I walked nearer and approached the group. One was doing the work of pruning while her cell phone was tucked between her ear and her shoulder. Another, the crew leader, was clearly a dynamic and good-natured woman as she chided the other workers and worked alongside them at their tasks.

And then I heard it – another woman, singing *fado*.

Fado is the Portuguese musical tradition that conveys the resignation and longing of the working class. The tradition goes way back – at least to the 1820s though probably much earlier – but it still resonates today. The *fado* I heard and recorded in the vineyards that day was sung by a woman named Maria Julia, who echoed the original recording by the legendary *fado* singer Amália Rodrigues.

On that particular day in 2013 in national politics, the country's Finance Minister had just resigned, public support for Portugal's austerity measures was in decline, and government debt had fallen sharply on the trading floor.

I don't know if Maria Julia and the rest of this crew knew or cared about those things. They knew they had this job to do, while the overall unemployment rate in Portugal hovered around 15%. For people younger than 25 years old, it was even worse at about 35%.

Given that environment, in vineyards where the labor is especially difficult and intense, *fado* seemed appropriate and Maria Julia's voice all the more poignant.

———

The migration of labor is like a pendulum shift, sometimes away from the agrarian lifestyle, and sometimes back toward it, back and forth over time and geography.

The migration of labor is also a basic question of too-high demand and too-low supply to meet it.

Which opens the door for matching the supply of workers with the demand of farms and estates. In some cases, like in New Zealand with the crew from Vanuatu, it's a government-sponsored program. In other cases, like the Portuguese man I mentioned in Champagne, it's a question of entrepreneurs taking the initiative.

In some cases, like Tasmania, it's a little of both.

Tasmania and New Zealand share many similarities. They are both grape-growing, wine-producing islands in the Pacific Ocean and, it turns out, they both also welcome immigrant labor from other parts of Asia to work their harvest – from Vanuatu for New Zealand, and from Thailand, Taiwan, Japan, and Korea for Tasmania.

In Tasmania, at this moment in time, crews of visiting vineyard workers are primarily comprised of young women. Some of them are students taking time off to travel for a few years, others are more experienced agricultural workers who grow and harvest not only grapes but other crops like cherries and apricots as well.

The crews are the brainchild of a reluctant entrepreneur named Nigel Mobbs, an Australian vegetable grower who created a company called HortForce. Mobbs and his wife were responding to the needs of their own business that were also the needs of other businesses nearby, including wineries. As an employment subcontractor, Mobbs recruits and trains the workers, organizers their travel and schedules, and he implements contracts, currently at AU$28.50 per hour to start.

The need – in New Zealand, Italy, France, Portugal, and elsewhere – is for crews of workers like this. Unlike those other countries, however, the women harvesters in Tasmania have organized their work in a noticeably different way. It's known as the "crab walk." Rather than travel from vine to vine, vertically up and down the rows, as is common around the world, the workers in Tasmania have recognized it is more efficient for them to travel sideways as they work, actually ducking from one row horizontally to the next, across the vineyard.

It looks like the difference between eating an ear of corn around its cob rather than from one end across to the other, typewriter style.

I've never known any other harvest workers to operate this way. I've also never known any other harvest crew being comprised almost entirely of young Asian women. Just like meeting the Vanuatu islanders with their rabbit, meeting these women in Tasmanian vineyards embodies the answer to the question of who harvests your grapes, and how they do it, as new people with new sets of eyes and skills approach the vines, knives in hand.

Jennifer Doyle, Vineyard Manager for Jansz Parish Vineyard, described an experienced supervisor named Miwa, who arrives at the vineyard with her crew already familiar with the layout and Jansz' preferred techniques for the task at hand.

"The formidable Miwa is a petite Japanese woman whose partner is Australian, so she is here for the long-term," Doyle said. "Miwa leads her crew of Thai, Japanese, Taiwanese, Chinese, and South Korean with courteous but clear and direct instruction. English is the common language."

Crew members come from varied backgrounds. Some are permanent residents of Tasmania, some are studying, and some are on working holidays. They work in pairs, opposite one another, on either side of the vine.

The HortForce grape pickers are supported by Jansz' own small group of "regular casuals," Bhutanese refugees with an agricultural background in their home country. They assist with tractor driving, Doyle said. They collect fully laden picking buckets and empty them into half-ton bins, and distribute empty buckets back to the picking team.

Doyle described Lok Thapa, an integral member of this team, as a "viticultural trainee with a voracious thirst for knowledge." His immense enthusiasm is both refreshing and rewarding, Doyle said, and he also assists in interpretation, "particularly for some of the more senior members of his community who have taken a little longer to adjust to conversing in the English language."

Neither Miwa nor Lok Thapa may be who you expect to find in the vineyards of Tasmania, and they may not be who you assumed picked the grapes that made the wine you're drinking. But it's their hunger – and the hunger driving the demand for the fruit that they pick – that traces the profile of what it took to bring a bottle of wine to your table.

Tasting Note: NV Jansz Premium Cuvée Sparkling Wine

Most of the vines that the workers in Tasmania harvest are either Pinot Noir or Chardonnay, in order to support the extremely strong demand there for sparkling wine grapes. Most of the grapes the Vanuatu islanders in New Zealand harvest are either Sauvignon Blanc or Pinot Noir, in order to support the demand for juice from those two grapes that Kiwi winemakers have built their market around.

Jansz' Premium Cuvée is a standard bearer of Australia's sparkling wine industry, especially given the quality reputation of Tasmania's cool climate fruit. Secondary fermentation takes place in the bottle, and the wine is aged on its lees for two years or more. The Pinot Noir component of the wine offers a hint of strawberry on the nose, and palate notes also include citrus, honeysuckle, and roasted nuts. Long, creamy finish with a touch of nougat sweetness.

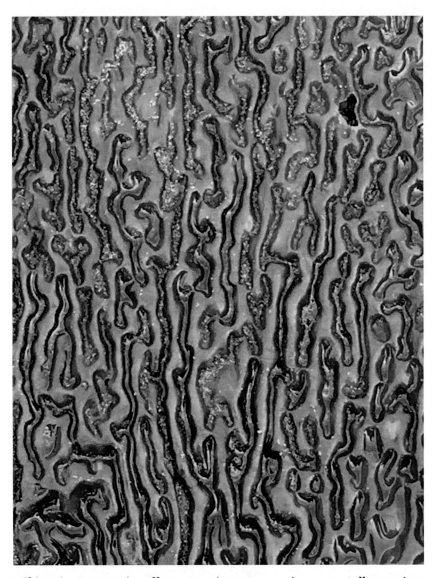

Hiking in Patagonia offers stunning macro views as well as micro views, such as this detail of seaweed kelp found on a beach near a glacier.

Chapter Five
How to Learn about Wine While
Hiking in Patagonia

Everything I know about wine writing I learned in Patagonia.

Okay maybe not *everything*.

But definitely some of the most important things.

Like the power of place, for one. And the insight to look behind the vines for another. The idea is to know the people who grow the grapes and who make the wines, and to find where this all happens.

Traveling to Patagonia – as strange as this sounds – underscored these lessons of wine writing. They were lessons in Where and Who, two of any writer's most pivotal interrogatives.

It wasn't as though I had to go to Patagonia – an almost grape-less region of Chile – to learn these lessons. But if you're going to choose a location for a classroom, Patagonia's not half bad.

———

Patagonia – along with Tasmania and the western coast of Scotland – seems to me like the edge of the earth. Which meant, of course, that I simply had to go.

Along the way we visited a penguin colony at the exact geographical point at the southern tip of South America where the Atlantic and the Pacific Oceans converge.

(It's down there. Way down there. As in, next-stop-Antarctica-down-there.)

We hiked along the beach past new baby sea lions and their mothers, and along a river where young male sea lions flexed their muscles in chest-to-chest battle against each other. We saw leopard seals (which were terrifying) and waterfalls during hikes (which were not) and plenty of the glacial geology that carved this portion of the earth. For the record, when glaciers melt or pieces collapse and shift, they sound like a groan of the gods that echoes and reverberates from here to the South Pole.

We had front row seats to it all.

The question is, how did any of this relate to the wines of Chile?

The answer is partly about the scenery, which provided the backdrop that – truly and wholly – sealed the geography of this place in my memory. The scenery informed, and still continues to inform, my understanding of Chilean wines. My memories of the trip were etched by the geography as much as the people of that place.

That's because Patagonia evokes the associations that the Chilean wine industry wants evoked, as a New World wine region that is also well-rooted in its cultural history.

Chile is a place of remarkably stunning natural beauty. It runs some 3000 miles from north to south, hugging the west coast of South America like the delicate, tucked-under hem of a hand-stitched couture lapel. Chile averages only 100 miles in width for its entire length, "as skinny as six o'clock," as my Dad would say. Its eastern border is the spine of the Andes Mountains. From Chile's northern tip where its boundary intersects with Peru and Bolivia, all the way south to the fjords of Patagonia, there is a diversity of ecologies that have honed and defined vineyards for hundreds of years.

Chile has also long been a destination for immigrants, especially from western European winemaking countries such as Spain and Italy. The immigrants planted roots there. And they planted vines. That history gives the current wine scene its heritage and much of its credibility, and it also influences the outlook toward export markets. A high percentage – some 70% by most counts – of Chile's agricultural production (including wine) is shipped abroad. Chile also scores coups with its working free trade agreements, especially in Asia, which make its wine exports a significantly less expensive option on the shelf.

Each of these factors is an important reference point, or landmark, in my writing about the wines of Chile. They are also secondary – to the people, that is, who solidified this information in my mind, who fleshed out the data so to speak.

Let me tell you about one of them.

––––

Cecilia Torres is petite, with an easy, friendly smile. It's mischievous, even. It tells you that she gets the joke.

But I was shy about approaching her. Not because I'm a particularly shy person (I'm usually not), but because she struck me as an elder stateswoman, and I wanted to do a little reconnaissance first – a little research into who she was – so that my conversation with her was respectful of her time and position.

I needn't have worried. Yes, Cecilia has been around a long time. Yes, she has earned the respect of her peers and the media, and the loyalty of her co-workers. And yes, she serves as a role model for the upcoming generation, both women and men.

"I listen to young people today," she told me, "and I think, 'I don't know anything!' They make me feel like I need to start all over again."

That would be too bad. Because what Cecilia has accomplished can't ever be erased: she has spent a lifetime studying the terroir of Maipo Alto, and one specific 20-hectare vineyard of Alto Jahuel in particular: 25 vintages (and counting) of 100% Cabernet Sauvignon from Casa Real. She understands the expression and subtlety of it the way that a hermit crab understands every nuance of its shell.

"It's either a crazy concept or it's a secure concept," she said about making the same wine from the same vineyard for 25 years. "Or maybe a combination of both."

The vineyard was planted in the 1970s, and Cecilia's first harvest as the winemaker was in 1989. Her goal was always to show individual harvests and vintages, by creating a wine that can age and be cellared.

Her Cabernet Sauvignon is very complex, very complete, and also very pure.

"It's very hard to save this concept," she said, especially with commercial marketing departments that try pushing her and the wine in different directions. "For 25 years I've had to defend the style of the Cab. If I could find a Merlot or a Cabernet Franc that was at the same level as the Cabernet Sauvignon, I'd be happy to blend it in. But so far I haven't seen it."

The complicated thing about what's left – a single varietal wine from a single vineyard – is that there isn't a lot of space to make it wrong.

Tasting Note: Casa Real Cabernet Sauvignon, from 2011, 2008 and 2005

Working with the same vineyard and the same grape year after year offers its consistencies, as well as its variabilities. Some years the Casa Real vineyard yields only 1000 cases. In other years, the most productive ones, it could be as much as 3500 cases. Recently she's been experimenting with fermenting in barrel and the percentage of new oak that's used.

For Cecilia, some harvests make her laugh and some make her cry. Each one has its own personality, but the persistent one is that Casa Real is what she calls a "calm and quiet" wine.

A vertical tasting is an excellent way to see how the consistencies and variabilities play themselves out year over year. Cecilia poured three Casa Real wines for me, from the 2005, 2008, and 2011 vintages. If I were to put it in the context of the duration of a meal, I'd serve them chronologically in reverse, from youngest to oldest: the very fresh 2011 with a cheese board to start, as though it were an *aperitivo*; then, with the first course, I'd serve the harmonious 2008; I'd save the 2005 for the rich main course.

2011

This vintage was the latest harvest of Cecilia's life. (The crew didn't start harvesting until April 30 which, in the southern hemisphere, is very late in the cycle.) She literally didn't answer the phone, and avoided the people pressing her for an answer about when and whether to start picking.

"The people from the vineyard wanted to kill me," she said. "But I just waited."

That patience led to a deep, complex wine with aromas of red and black fruits like plums and cherries as well as sweeter notes of vanilla and coffee. It is a baby, still, potent with layers of oak and tobacco and the promise of many years ahead of it.

2008

Cecilia has tears in her eyes when we try this wine. Why?

"It rained when it had to," she said. The temperatures weren't too low or too high: they were moderate and consistent throughout the whole cycle of the grapes' growth and ripening.

If the 2011 were a fresh, "spring time" wine, the 2008 represents autumn. The 2008 was a low-yield vintage, with only 1000 cases produced from the vineyard. It is younger and greener but also elegant, with notes of blackberries and black currants, and strong but not overwhelming concentration.

2005

If I were serving a main course of meat – lamb, say, or turkey at Thanksgiving – and I were to make a sauce to serve with this wine, I'd flavor it with strawberry, cranberry, star anise, also a touch of mint. My tasting notes for this wine parallel those ingredients: rich spices, with red and black fruits. The tannins are nine years young, so to speak, and so soft, balanced, and elegant that you'd never guess this wine was aged in 100% oak.

This wine makes me want to sit down. It makes me want to find That Person. It makes me want to have That Conversation.

Note to Self

One day soon I will write an article called "Life Lessons from Women Winemakers," and here is the quote I will use from Cecilia Torres:

> You need to be careful and meticulous. That's fundamental. You also need to know how to wait, and to wait for the unexpected. The Casa Real wine takes three years to come to market, and we have to be able to wait for that. Why not apply the same thinking to your life too?

Cecilia belongs to a group of women I have met in the wine industry in the past few years, who stand out to me as much for their professional accomplishments as for the strength of their character. They have been around the block, so to speak. They are wise. They look you in the eye. They know their opinions and express them clearly. You get the sense that they *see* you. They are polite, of course, but they'd rather get to the point. Because that's when it gets good.

Octopi strung up along the shoreline of Santorini help create the
perfect backdrop for the perfect wine on a perfect day.

Chapter Six
How to Protect Wine from
Greece's Economic Crisis

One sunny day in July, at lunchtime, we drove in Petros Vamvakousis' little blue car from the very top of the hill, on the very top of the Greek island of Santorini, down and down.

Down switchbacks.

Down narrow roads crowded with people.

Down almost to the bottom, where a little set of shops and restaurants clung to the edge of the land along the water.

We parked the car into a tight spot along a narrow, nearly vertical row of cars – one of those high-angle situations where a parking brake is imperative (the whole island is like that) and we walked the rest of the way.

We walked past the octopi strung up, as on clotheslines, one alongside the other. We passed one seaside restaurant, crossed a tiny footbridge (inches from the water, no guiderails), and continued past another until we got to the place where Petros carefully chose a whole fish from the day's catch to be cooked for us.

The weather was warm, the meal was fish, we were in an outdoor restaurant along a Mediterranean coastline. In other words, we were smack in the middle of the perfect conditions for a white wine that's fresh and cool, and very much from this place.

Petros, it turns out, makes such a wine. The server – dressed very casually and indistinguishably from everyone else in the restaurant – brought Petros' 2013 Moschofilero to the table.

Petros is a winemaker for Boutari, a major producer in Greece. Ioanna Vamvakouri, another winemaker who works with Petros at Boutari, joined us for lunch. Ioanna talked about a conversation she'd had when visiting California. Someone, another winemaker, had asked her "what she does" with her wines.

"I don't do much," she remembers saying. "I help to grow the grapes. I pick them at the right time, and I get them into the winery. And that's about it."

She didn't say who it was, but she did say that the California winemaker seemed very surprised at what sounded to him like a radically non-interventionist approach.

We laughed about that conversation, partly because Ioanna, though opinionated, is not often considered the most radical person in the room. We also laughed about the conversation, because it reflects a very different set of expectations of a winemaker. That particular winemaker in California thought that there was a lot to *do* with grapes and wine, while Ioanna thought that, for the most part, the grapes do their own thing and her job is to simply stand by and let them.

It's the difference between hands-on and hands-off winemaking, between thinking you can do something about the wine and thinking it's pretty much out of your control.

———

There was much that was idyllic about that lunchtime scenario. The location. The food. The conversation. The leave-it-to-the-gods approach to winemaking.

You'd have thought that the cares of the world were far, far away. Yet everywhere you looked in Greece, from Athens to Crete to the mainland to right there on Santorini, there was also a sense of *strain*. Resources were strained. Public amenities were strained. People, many of whom were jobless, were strained.

They still are.

Greece was – and still is – struggling its way through a deep and pervasive economic crisis, and prospects for recovery have long seemed dim, or at least a lifetime of belt-tightening away.

56

And yet.

And yet there was this wine, in this idyllically beautiful place.

It seemed on the one hand like a complete oxymoron: something beautiful emerging from such strain and difficulty. But, on the other hand, it was totally logical: of course this wine emerged from this place, just as it had been doing for many, many centuries. Wine production in Greece is an ancient and well-oiled practice whose continuity even during difficult times is renowned. The players may change, but the wine persists.

Resources in Greece right then were strained, but its people – the Who of winemaking there – are famously resourceful.

I wanted to trace the reasons for it. I wanted to know not only the Who but also the Where. I wanted to see this world of Greece, in this particular moment of financial difficulty, through the lens of the wine glass that was in front of me.

It wouldn't necessarily help me get my head around the big picture math or the interest rates or the data of the crisis, but that glass of wine could provide some insight into the crisis at a human scale.

———

Ioanna's approach to winemaking is to interfere as little as possible with the natural flow of the grape-growing process. For other farmers on the island, that natural flow includes complementary crops likes olives, fava beans, peaches, tomatoes, and eggplant, which are integrated into the plantings of vines. It's a complementary mix that yields a supply of healthy and sustainable produce that is enviable to urban inhabitants of Athens who, at the worst moments of Greece's recent economic crisis, struggled to find or afford food to eat.

The availability of produce on their families' farms is exactly what's enticed a trail of Greece's young people back to the rural areas. Even though many of them left the farms a few years earlier, certain that a university education and urban employment were their ticket out of the physically demanding lifestyle.

They got the education, but not the employment.

There was no counting on Greece's government debt crisis, and an unemployment rate that rivals what was experienced in the U.S. in the 1930s during the Great Depression.

—————

A few days before that lunch on Santorini, I'd met another winemaker, this time on the island of Crete.

Vivi Papaspirou described how younger generations, like herself and even younger, grew up on farms and vineyards but never thought that it would be their work. Trying to break away from the family farm, in search of education and professional opportunities elsewhere, had become the norm.

"We all grew up thinking we'd work in offices," Vivi said. "It's an adjustment to think we'd be working with our hands. The people who work the harvest now are still getting used to the idea."

That's because, as Vivi said, "there is no program on your PC for growing grapes."

It's an adjustment, to say the least, to shift from a mentality of classroom and office work into a farming lifestyle. Yet that's exactly what's happening, as the number of new producers has increased sharply in the recent years of Greece's crisis. In the Naoussa region alone, in northern Greece, the number of producers has grown from just a handful a few years ago to more than 25 today.

Yet, partly as a lingering sentiment of not expecting to work on the family farm, young people are much more likely to study as enologists (the people who make the wine) rather than as viticulturalists (the people who grow the grapes to make the wine). It is the difference between working inside the winery and outside of it, in the fields.

Balancing those two trends – a rush of new producers on the one hand, and a shortage of experienced viticulturalists on the other – will be a challenge and an opportunity moving forward.

Vivi, Petros and Ioanna have front-row seats to those developments. Petros, for example, now consults for a new boutique vineyard whose owner is sparing no cost for plantings and production.

And Ioanna was recently elected to a seat on an environmental commission that's considering the implications of a major highway on Santorini.

A major highway cutting through Santorini?

The kneejerk response to anyone who's been there, and experienced even a fraction of the appeal of the island's craggy, haphazard geography, is *No*.

Just... no.

No way.

Part of Santorini's charm *is* the crowded, narrow two-lane roads that cling to the sides of the mountains. A multi-lane highway would negatively and irreversibly impact both the ecological and cultural environments of the island.

The argument in favor of the highway is that it would handle the hoards of tourists visiting the island. And there are, indeed, hoards of them. Try making your way through the massive crowds arriving by huge ferries and cruiseships at the pier, and you'll be forgiven for wondering, Crisis? What economic crisis?

Still, Santorini's tourist appeal may be its own demise.

The island's tourism industry insulates it to a large extent from the financial difficulties seen elsewhere in Greece. Yet at the local level, officials are at a pivot point of deciding what role the wine industry can play within its thriving tourist trade, which has the power and momentum to overshadow the less lucrative wine category.

Ioanna, with her non-interventionist philosophy and seat on the environmental commission, will have a say in the direction the officials pivot. But you get the sinking feeling that she may well be in the minority.

If the infrastructure developments proceed, if the multi-lane highway is built, the progress of tourists through the island may indeed flow more easily.

But then – then – the Where of the experience of wine on Santorini will change.

I don't know how these details would affect the flavor of the wine, if there were no switchbacks, if there were no two-lane roads, if the grade of the hill where you park your car didn't necessitate the emergency brake.

But I do know that they set the scene, and the atmosphere affects the aroma and the taste of the wine too.

In the coming years, I will also be curious to see how the "new Who" of Greece's wine industry carve their own place into its history. How will their education, even if it wasn't in viticulture or enology, affect their approach? Will they hold onto the traditional ways? Will they be more open-minded to new technologies?

Whatever the outcome, the glass of wine from Greece that you hold in your hand ten or even five years from now will have a very different story to tell about its Where and Who than the glass of wine you hold today. Both are snapshots of an industry in flux.

———

To find yourself in exactly the right place at exactly the right moment – and with a glass of wine in front of you that you are thoroughly enjoying – underscores the value of *timing* when it comes to discovering that you, too, are hungry for wine.

This happened for me on the island of Santorini, one sunny July day at lunchtime. It was a perfect day, in a perfect place, we'd found the perfect wine, and the echo of my motivation for this book reverberated quietly and deeply all around me.

This was more of what I wanted in my life.

This was my hunger for wine.

I imagined it spreading into the glasses of each person at the table, as if that hunger poured literally from the bottle of wine we shared. My hunger for wine was met, in that place with that wine at that time with those people.

It was *enough*. I was full.

Tasting Note: 2013 Boutari Moschofilero

Moschofilero isn't likely to launch deep philosophical debate about the growth or demise of the Greek economy. But it is an indicator and an emblem of it – of something that's working right, of a reliable cash crop, of a long-rooted local grape that, despite its light body and fresh acidity, is nonetheless a stalwart workhorse of the wine industry here.

Plus it's perfect – perfect – for easy, companionable, laughing lunches on a sunny day, seated at a table full of fish dishes, at an open-aired restaurant alongside the Santorini coastline.

Grown primarily on Greece's Peloponnese peninsula, Moschofilero is a pink-skinned grape with floral, often lemony aromas similar to Muscat and lighter Gewürztraminers. Hints of white rose and sea salt also show through on the nose. It's the wine's refreshing acidity that's suited so perfectly to white fish dishes and the warm open air of summer.

Fishermen prepare their nets in the early morning, near Suvla winery on Turkey's Gallipoli peninsula.

Chapter Seven
How to Market Wine When
It's Forbidden to Market Wine

In Greece, during the last chapter, I used a glass of wine as a lens into that country's massive economic crisis. Wine is a sliver of what's happening there, one small click on the kaleidoscope of the big picture, but a useful one nonetheless because it's one I understand and can relate to.

In Turkey, in this chapter, I'll use a glass of wine as a similar lens into something similarly massive: an entire country, a major wine-producing country even, whose politics and culture are to me mysterious and largely unknown.

Just like Greece, Turkey is at a pivot point on many levels – geography, religion, history, and politics, to name a few. It is a crossroads and a forum where some of today's global debates are enacted and dissected, from energy security to government-controlled media to women's rights.

Visiting the wine regions of Turkey wasn't even my first experience there: years earlier I'd been to both Istanbul and Sanliurfa, in the southeast near the border with Syria. There in particular I saw how complex the relationship is between tradition and modernization.

Still, my understanding of Turkey was (is) minimal. I was looking for a way *in*, and that way again was wine.

It started on a beach on Turkey's Gallipoli peninsula, looking out onto waters that were once tinged red with the blood of soldiers.

——

Selim Zafer Ellialti, the founder and owner of nearby Suvla Wines, had brought us there.

It was the site of one of the most historically significant battles of World War I, yet I had never even heard of it.

The Battle of Gallipoli is seen as a defining moment in the history of the nation of Turkey – not to mention the national consciousness of Australia and New Zealand, their thwarted opponents who were fighting on behalf of the Allies – yet I had to Google it on our way there.

It was humbling, to say the least.

It was also indicative of everything else I didn't know about Turkey, specifically its wine production and the way that current political regulations restricted the marketing and promotion of wine within Turkey's own borders.

"I had no idea," was a phrase that ran through my head over and over.

But I was there to learn.

———

Selim called it a "hero wine."

I agree – the 2011 Suvla Reserve Petit Verdot-Karasakiz is exactly that.

Yet he came to the wine quietly, after our group had tasted a dozen or so other wines from his estate on the Gallipoli Peninsula.

We were at dinner, about eight of us at the table, part of a dining area set between the winery and a very chic shop that sells Suvla wines alongside books, a carefully curated selection of beautiful housewares, and various gourmet food items that are also packaged on site.

The shop is disorienting at first, with its eye-catching displays and abundance of visual, tactile, and aromatic luxuries. It is a place of finesse, and design, and innate pleasure. It is a place that prizes detail, and quality, and appreciation of sensory indulgence.

It is a place, in other words, that is almost perfectly contrary to the tone that the Turkish government was trying to impose during the time of my visit, at least when it comes to wine (and any other form of alcohol while they're at it).

Since June 2013 there have been regulations within Turkey against the promotion of alcohol – meaning no websites, no brochures, no marketing materials, no communications the way we normally think about wine communications.

There is to be no writing about wine, neither good nor bad. There is to be no celebration of it, even when the wine (like this one) reflects well on the country's agricultural efforts and entrepreneurial initiatives.

This is a problem.

Winery owners like Selim and his colleagues at wineries throughout Turkey face the same challenges. Many have found success within the domestic market, where most Turkish wineries sell upwards of 95% of their production.

When they first heard of the government regulations, it sent them into a tailspin, especially new and small producers (like Suvla) who are just getting a toehold in the market. Suddenly, the reliable and successful avenues of promoting their wines – to 95% of their consumer base – was no longer available to them.

The tailspin was the kneejerk reaction.

Then there were the protests, which continue still.

Then, with their backs to the wall, there is the creativity that comes from necessity.

———

How do you market wine when it's forbidden to market wine?

Two creative responses to the regulations – word of mouth (WOM) and selling direct-to-consumer (DTC) – are, in a way, a return to the essentials of marketing.

Even though they can't advertise as wine events per se, several wineries continue to host dinners and events – at their wineries, in private homes, and at venues both within Istanbul and in more rural areas. Spreading the news about the events, however, becomes a question of quiet (if sometimes viral) word of mouth: it starts with one fan or admirer of a winery or brand, who tells friends, who invites others to the event, and so on.

Vinkara Winery, for example, participates in regular, popular, and closed-group dinners of 14 people in Istanbul. Two seats are taken by Vinkara representatives, and the remainder are filled by the host who has invited a tight network of friends and colleagues into his home. There is no explicit invitation, and no mention that wine will be served. But it's understood – wink, wink – that Vinkara wines will be served and discussed.

Other wineries host larger events that piggy-back on the popularity of food and chefs. Barbare Winery, located about 1.5 hours outside Istanbul along the newly-formed tourist trail called the Thrace Wine Route (Trakya Bağ Rotasi in Turkish), hosts wine dinners featuring a popular chef from the city. They utilize WOM via social media – particularly Instagram – to capitalize on the visual beauty of their location and details of their events.

DTC, or selling wine directly to the consumer, is another creative response to the government regulations. Can Ortabaş, owner of Urla winery near Izmir, expects some 60,000 visitors to knock on his winery door this year alone, partly as drop-in guests and partly as participants in corporate events and private parties. That flow of guests yields what, for Turkey, is an astronomically high 40% of sales as DTC.

Ortabaş executes a strategy of what's good for Urla-the-winery is good for Urla-the-locality. Both the winery and its geographical region share the same name; calling your winery "Urla" is the equivalent of calling it "Sonoma" or "Friuli." Of course Ortabaş wants his own winery to succeed, but the bigger vision is for the region to succeed, the way that Robert Mondavi in the 1960s in California saw that the success of Napa overall was also good for the success of Mondavi individually.

"My dream is to have 100 wineries on this little peninsula," Ortabaş said.

Urla's audience is broadly international and taps into the popularity of Izmir as a destination for European tourists. The writing is on the wall for Turkey's wineries today: they need to appeal to that international component.

———

Turkey does not have a long tradition of wine consumption. That is, its tradition is as ancient as Georgia's and Armenia's, if you consider archaeological evidence of amphorae and ancient literature mentioning local wines. But popular consumption within a contemporary context is still finding its way.

If it's a long tradition, it's also a broken one. And that's the catch.

When you can't talk about your wines, when you can't introduce them to new consumers in your most immediate, easiest-accessible market, the longevity of your business is obviously endangered.

Promoting Turkish wine *outside* Turkey, however, is perfectly acceptable. It is as though Turkey's government is happy for people to enjoy any form of alcohol, as long as those people are not Turkish and residing within their borders.

Which perhaps helps to explain why Selim Ellialti came to his award-winning wine quietly that night at dinner, when it came time to choose what to pour next.

"Maybe next we'll try this one," he said, and passed the bottle around to his largely international group of guests.

It was the 2011 Suvla Reserve Petit Verdot-Karasakiz.

The "hero wine."

It's a hero wine not because it successfully merges national and international classifications, though it does that with its blend of Petit Verdot and Karasakiz.

It's a hero wine not because it's won the winery critical global acclaim, though it did that too, including the Grand Gold Medal at the 2014 Concours Mondial du Bruxelles.

This is a "hero wine" because a journalist in Istanbul wrote about it, defying those government regulations against the promotion of alcohol within Turkey. "Promotion" includes writing about wine, and the journalist risked his job, a fine, and the potential shut-down of his newspaper. He risked all that not once but twice, the second time in response to the public reaction to his first post.

This is a hero wine because it inspired that kind of defiance.

This is a hero wine because it won that Grand Gold Medal two years in a row, which is something no other wine – from anywhere – has done.

This is a hero wine because of how that represents Turkey, and especially the state of the Turkish wine industry today.

Because another response to the government regulations against the promotion of alcohol is the one the journalist chose: defiance. That's where the irony comes in.

Despite the violation against the regulation, the journalist is still writing, still working, still at his desk.

That's the thing about this moment in the history of Turkish wine.

They let him be, despite the violation of the regulation. It's like the sale and consumption of alcohol in retail shops – it still happens. And restaurants still sell alcohol.

For now.

Tasting Note: 2011 Suvla Reserve Petit Verdot-Karasakiz

It poured deep and dark in the glass, like midnight tinged with violet. Some of us smelled mocha and dried cherry; for others it was cinnamon, walnut, and chocolate. I smelled all of those things. But for

me, what makes this Suvla wine so memorable was its mouth feel –
structured and supple, with a powerfully strong core yet elegant
edges.

If the physique of a hero could be corralled into a glass, and distilled,
this would be it.

It was the mouth feel of this wine that won me over, that makes it a
wine worth savoring. But the narrative makes it a wine worth
memorializing.

The vineyard manager at Château Marsyas, Bargylus' sister property in the Bekaa Valley of Lebanon, drives a water tank through the vineyards.

Chapter Eight
How to Make Wine When
Your Country is at War

It was the winter of 2010, at a fancy tasting, with fancy wine, in a fancy hotel in Paris.

Producers from all over the world who worked with the host of the event – a well-known consulting winemaker – stood behind their assigned tables, pouring samples of their wines for the trade and media who attended.

Off to one side was a table with two guys who were... different.

Which means, naturally, that I made a beeline straight for them.

They poured me a taste of their red wine in the glass I held out to them. Our first conversation went something like this:

Me: So you're making wine? In, uh, Syria?

Them: Exactly!

Me: Why are you making wine in Syria?

Them: We love wine! And we think everyone should drink more of it.

Me: I agree. Completely. But... Syria?

[They paused, looked harder at me, and then continued with considerably more seriousness.]

Them: We want to show the world that our country is about more than its regime.

———

This was before Syria blew up.

I kept this producer on my radar in the years since then, and in 2013 I had a chance to visit them in Beirut. Neither they (nor their consulting winemaker, Stéphane Derenoncourt) had been able to cross the border into Syria to access their own property – Château Bargylus, near Latakia – since November of 2012.

Yet they were still making wine from that vineyard. And that summer, at another fancy tasting, this time in the fanciest district of the souk in Beirut, I had the chance to taste their newest release.

A lively group had gathered on that mild June evening. It was more of a consumer crowd this time than the trade and media crowd in Paris, and this time the tasting was focused particularly on the recently released white wine of Château Bargylus.

We gathered outside La Cave de Joël Robuchon, the Beirut wine shop of one of Paris' most revered chefs. A variety of cheeses were served. Guests – from business people to artists to engineers – engaged in enthusiastic, animated conversation. The Bargylus Blanc, a blend of Chardonnay and Sauvignon Blanc, was poured into glasses that clinked and were raised in toasts and celebration of its new release.

The setting could have been Paris, with wines from Bordeaux. Or San Francisco, with wines from Napa. Or Rome, with wines from Tuscany. But it was Beirut, with wines from Syria.

With Syria's civil war literally at their doorstep, the launch of a new wine in Beirut may seem insensitive or, worse, unmindful of the tragedy and casualties of the conflict. Yet the perseverance and determination required to bring this particular wine to market underscores the grim irony that, despite the chaos of civil war, there are moments of relative consistency.

Despite the war, people continue with the work of their lives.

For consultant Stéphane Derenoncourt and especially for the Saadé family, who own wineries in both Syria and the Bekaa Valley of Lebanon, that work is wine.

———

"We have to keep going," said Karim Saadé, whose family owns these wineries as well as several other regional interests in real estate and finance. We had stepped inside to the back room of the wine shop, where I interviewed him and his brother Sandro for a last-minute assignment for BBC Radio.

"We've gone through so many hardships, as a family, as a people," Karim said. "It's not the first time. It won't be the last. You need to stay, to persevere. Through resiliency, you need to get to the best."

The Saadés are a Christian family with a long history in Syria. Karim and Sandro's grandfather was one of the largest industrialists in Syria when the family's assets were seized in the 1960s.

"He had to rebuild everything outside Syria, in Lebanon and Europe," Sandro said into my phone, which was the only recording equipment I had available. "Our challenge has been to come back to where we came from."

Establishing Château Bargylus has been part of that return.

The estate is located on the slopes of the Al-Ansariyah mountains in the northwestern part of Syria. Since 2006, and in partnership with Derenoncourt, Bargylus has produced high-quality red and white wines in a very unique and very challenging, environment. At an altitude of 900 meters and an orientation facing the Mediterranean Sea, Bargylus benefits from a fresh climate with high temperatures during the day and cooler ones at night.

As this is the only modern wine producer in Syria, it is difficult to describe the wines in comparison to close peers.

Even though there is a long history of winemaking in Syria, there are no varieties left from those ancient times. Still, Derenoncourt said he wanted to make something that is "very much from the Middle East, with spice and citrus."

For Derenoncourt, who also consults on Bargylus' sister property (Château Marsyas) in the Bekaa Valley of Lebanon, Syria offers "something very special."

At Bargylus in Syria, the vines face more of a struggle because of soil and climatic conditions.

At Bargylus the vines fight the humidity, while the Bekaa is hot and very dry.

At Bargylus the climate is similar in some ways to Bordeaux. A grape such as Cabernet Sauvignon, for example, may not ripen until quite late. Grapes at Château Marsyas may ripen an entire month earlier.

The altitude is nearly the same, about 900 meters, but Marsyas is located between two mountains.

All of those factors impact production. Bargylus' yield is smaller, normally 40,000 to 45,000 bottles per year, while at Marsyas in Lebanon it is 55,000 bottles per year.

———

Limited production is not, of course, the only difficulty facing Derenoncourt and the Saadé family as they try to grow grapes in Syria. The war has made even the simplest matters of production exponentially more difficult and precarious.

Derenoncourt himself hadn't physically visited the property in the two years before I interviewed him in 2013, since the beginning of the war. The day-to-day operation of the winery is in the hands of the vineyard manager, who started with Derenoncourt and the Saadés literally from the ground up, from their very first plantings during the first decade of this century.

"We manage the estate by phone, email, and photos," said Derenoncourt. "During the ripening season when I am in Lebanon, the grapes from Syria come by taxi. Everything is very complex."

The adjustments the Saadés have had to make in order to continue producing wine in Syria would press the limits of most businessmen's patience. For example, they continue to pay the salaries of their employees at the pre-conflict rate, even though the Syrian currency has plummeted. The Saadés need their employees to stay; they're the same employees who have been with the winery since it began, and trained vineyard workers in this part of the world are not so easy to come by.

It was an important decision, Sandro said. But it was more than just business. "It created a sense of cohesion and purpose. We're acting like a family in times of distress and problems. This is what *terroir* is about as well."

Preserving *terroir* in the context of Syria's current situation means instituting unusual processes at harvest, the most sensitive time of the year for winemaking. For example, the grapes are placed on ice and driven by hired car across the border to Beirut for tasting and analysis. A truck carrying empty glass bottles, which were to be filled with the newest vintage, was once stopped at the border for two weeks. The winery's lawyer, official paperwork in hand, was enlisted to travel with the truck.

Each of these obstacles adds significantly to the cost of carrying out the business of wine.

But the most difficult part of operating Château Bargylus at that moment, Sandro said, was convincing their employees that there is a future for them in Syria.

"We're seeing people every day who are leaving their homes, their work, and everything they've done so far. Hopefully this will stop and things will get better, on all sides."

———

For Karim and Sandro, whether they would continue to produce wine in these circumstances was a no-brainer.

"The work right now is not usual," Sandro said. "Our main concern is to continue producing high quality wine in the current circumstances. We are not interested in producing wine if we are not able to do exceptional work with each vintage, so I hope we can continue in these conditions. That's the hard work to come, but not impossible."

His brother Karim agrees. "We want this land to be able to give something to the world that will be very much a quality product," he said. "People will judge, but this is our aim."

Tasting Note: 2012 Château Bargylus White

Back at the launch tasting that summer evening, at the souk in Beirut, many guests walked away having purchased several bottles of the newest release of Château Bargylus. Serving the wine on their tables at home is the final step of a long, arduous process involving a distinct commitment to the *terroir* of the land of Syria.

The wine is full and luscious on the palate, made from almost half-and-half Chardonnay and Sauvignon Blanc. In the glass the wine shimmers yellow with a touch of light green tonality. The aromas are pronounced, with citrus and herbal notes, especially lime and mint. The finish carries a fresh pluck of minerality, exhibited as bright acidity and lingering mouthfeel.

Getting the Story

Traveling in Lebanon, near the border with Syria, at the beginning of June 2013 may not have been the safest decision of my life. But I was chasing a story, and that chase has made me question how far I'm willing to go – geographically, emotionally, and psychologically – to get it.

There was a story here, and I wanted it. But it was not about the wine per se. It was about people as well as business and politics, and my initial questions when I met the Saadé family in Lebanon were along the lines of, How do you operate a business when your country is at war? And, how do you convince your workers to stay on the land rather than join the flood of refugees? How are other producers of wine in the Middle East affected by the conflict in Syria?

It was an unusual, and potentially provocative, story. Even before I left the US for Lebanon, I was getting some pushback. "It is difficult for me to speak about wine in Syria," one of my sources said, "given the terrible tragedy that we are suffering in front of the world unable to care." This was an Italian priest, long active at a monastery in Syria, who was speaking from Florence where he was living in exile.

It was certainly a fair point. But I explained – to this source and several others – that my article was starting with people who wanted to show the world that Syria is about more than its regime, and that I wanted to show a side of Syria that is unexpected. The response was silence. Maybe they didn't get it. Or maybe they just didn't believe me. But I had to go and see for myself.

My personal anxiety before I left the US for Lebanon was much more acute than when I actually got there. Partly it was a question of the unknown; I had never been there before. Partly it was the security issues and the US State Department's travel advisory. Partly it was the reaction of every one of my American friends and family, which was, without variation, Lebanon? Are you sure?

No, I wasn't sure. I was anxious too.

But I went anyway.

I had traveled in the Arab World before, in the Middle East and northeastern Africa as well. I had a solid frame of reference. I was aware of the danger, I thought, and my eyes were open.

Then I arrived, finally, in Lebanon. I landed in Beirut, and traveled in the Bekaa Valley. I listened and I watched, and listened some more, so that I could write.

I wrote about the motivations of businessmen, and their determination to persevere. I wrote about how people -- from Syria, Lebanon, Israel, and Tunisia -- demonstrate in their own ways that their countries are about more than their politics. Or that they would like them to be.

I wrote, in other words, about life. Another part of life in the Middle East than what we usually see in the media, to be sure, but life nonetheless. And the near reality of death.

In other words, I got the story.

But my *pursuit* of it is what gave me pause. Why did I want it so badly? Why was I so determined to get this particular story from that particular place at this particular time? Why was I – why am I – drawn so powerfully to a war zone?

There was the adrenaline and sense of adventure, for sure. That was part of it.

Part of it was the opportunity to tell an unusual story. As a writer I'm hungry for compelling insight that is not black and white or hard and fast but that is somehow true nonetheless.

Part of it was that I was looking for the slivers of humanity. Even though I'm properly outfitted with a journalist's radar for objectivity, and a business sense for what motivates decisions of commerce, I realize that my heart is looking for even the smallest portion of hope and humaneness.

And part of it is that I know in my heart that conflict, and hopefully resolution, is an integral part of the work of my life moving forward.

As I tweeted from the Beirut airport on my way home, my internal axis has effectively tilted a few degrees truer. I credit this to the people of Lebanon, if not to their politics. My axis has tilted a few degrees more aware, too, to slivers of humanity discovered where we aren't conditioned to find them.

Note: Portions of this chapter previously appeared in *Decanter*, *The Atlantic*, and DailyBeast.com.

The statues of the Abbazia di Rosazzo overlook the landscape and the vineyards of Livio Felluga's Friuli.

Chapter Nine
How to Plant Vines
in Order to Plant Roots

The map on the label of Livio Felluga wines has become a visual icon in the vast encyclopedia of Italian wines.

You can see why.

It is immediately recognizable. It is unique. It is a graphical constant that binds together a diverse range of wines.

But there is *something else* about this map label.

It wasn't imagined in a contemporary artist's studio. It isn't the winning image of a marketer's array of mock-ups. No focus group was convened.

It was, instead, found several decades ago in an antiques shop by Livio Felluga himself, who decided to use it on the labels of his wines. He did this for two reasons, the first practical and the second much more profound.

First, to differentiate his bottles from others in the area. And second, to show without question that these wines come from this specific place that the map represents: the region of Friuli, in northeastern Italy. Friuli was once part of Austria, and it was once Venetian. It once belonged to the people of the mountains, and it once belonged to the people of the sea.

It's a long story.

But with this map, Livio owned the decision to let the label represent every ragged edge and hollow cavern and lush meadow of the region that his is home.

Because Friuli is where Livio Felluga planted vines in order to plant roots.

———

The *something else* about the map label derives from the decision to repurpose a manuscript drawing.

Ancient and medieval manuscript drawings of a landscape *evoke* rather than represent; they *suggest* places and contours; and they allow for a certain amount of playful and imaginative "filling in the gaps" with diagrams or drawings of fantastical creatures in order to explain the unknown parts of the then-known universe.

The irony is that the creator of the original manuscript, hundreds of years ago, probably drew with almost as much certainty as mapmakers drew in more recent times. Although you'd think that more contemporary mapmakers could be much more specific and detailed, the delineations of one place and another weren't always so clear.

That's because the landscape of Felluga wines – the landscape, that is, of Friuli – has long been a contested corner of the earth.

Friuli, today, is a region of northeastern Italy. Slovenia lies to the east, Austria to the north, the Veneto to the south and west, and the Adriatic Sea to the south. The Alps also play a major role of geological definition.

Friuli, in other words, is a region at a crossroads. Over the years, it's been a crossroads of politics, commerce, culture, geography, and war. Friuli, Livio's son Andrea says, is a region that never had only one identity. It's been Venetian. Austrian. Friulian. They are Sea People. They are Mountain People. In Friuli, he says, "the meeting of different identities brings out the highest expression of them all."

———

Sometimes being hungry for wine means being hungry for the *place* of it.

Livio Felluga knows that the geography of the land *matters*.

He knows it in a way that inhabitants know it, inhabitants who have seen their own property change political allegiance over and over.

He knows it in a way that children of war know it. He was born during the throes of World War One, after which is home region was ceded by Austria to Italy.

And he knows it in a way that farmers and winemakers know it.

He knows it, and he built his wines around it.

Livio's first vintage was in 1956, seven years before the official launch of Italy's DOC system of identifying and protecting wines' provenance. Already by then he had a keen sense of the historical resonance that the landscape offered.

He grew up in a winemaking family in Istria, in what is now Croatia, and spent his youth opening markets for the wines (Malvasia and Refosco, specifically) in the nearby port city of Trieste as well as in the smaller towns and villages of Friuli. If you were to look on a map from that time, the towns would have been called names like Medana, and Cosana, and San Martin di Quisca.

Wine has always been part of Livio, in all its stages, from growing the vines to selling the wine. After World War II, he would not let it go, his son Andrea says. "It would have been easier. But he would have had to sacrifice his essence."

Livio's family lost their interests in Istria during the war but, seeing farmers abandon their land for post-conflict work and livelihoods in the cities, he knew that land in Friuli was cheap. In 1955 he purchased the first vineyards that would eventually grow to more than 330 acres' worth – and 300 distinct parcels – in the Collio and Colli Orientali hills of Friuli.

There are lifetimes of history and narrative in those few phrases – "his family lost their interests in Istria during the war" and "he purchased his first vineyards" – and I do not mean to gloss over their significance. But for the moment we can rely on these phrases to indicate a pivotal moment, when Livio transitioned from pre-war Istria to the start of something new in Friuli.

The thread that connects those two moments, the thread that persists through the pivot and on into today, is wine.

Wine, he says, is what has "always put bread on our table."

Choosing to settle in Friuli, to put vines and roots down in a place of such crossroads, is something that Livio had to do, according to Andrea Felluga. "He needed to settle, he needed a home, a place he could say he was from. He wanted his wines to have a definite origin and he wanted everyone to know it, which is why he chose the label he chose."

————

Let me go back to the map label, to the manuscript drawing found in an antiques store that has come to define one of Italy's most notable wine brands despite the inherent vagueness of its original iteration.

Sometimes, graphically, a few angled lines of the map label suggest hills, and slopes. Some are steeper than others. Others are alone, or in groups. You get the idea of rises and falls. You get the idea that, if you were to run your hand over this landscape, it would feel rough. It would bumble along. It would snag here and smooth out there.

It is a place with *texture*.

Sometimes, graphically, there are buildings, or at least the suggestions of buildings. A church, maybe. A farmhouse, maybe.

Once in a while there is water – a river or a stream or the tributaries that carve the landscape into so many segments of discernible earth.

Occasionally on the map labels there are place names. Maybe they're in Italian, maybe they're of Latin origin, maybe they're in local dialect. I can't tell. They're names like Ramanddo. Faedis. Torreano. Platiso. Sedilis. For some people, at some point in time, they may have served to orient. For me, today, they are reference points the way that

Atlantis is a reference point. It may or may not exist, but I am grateful for the fantastical need it fulfills.

For Livio Felluga, the map labels fulfilled a commercial need as well: he wanted to distinguish his wines and the focused winemaking techniques that he innovated in the region. He wanted to stamp the wines, in other words, as being not just from any place but from *this* place.

Tasting Note: 2013 Livio Felluga Terre Alte

The Livio Felluga estate grows grapes and produces wines (including several single varietal wines) that are anchored to this specific place. Friulano. Sauvignon Blanc. Pinot Grigio. Refosco dal Peduncolo Rosso.

Now, and as of 1981, they have also produced a wine called Terre Alte. Today it's widely regarded as one of Italy's finest white wines.

Terre Alte, first made some 25 years after Livio's first vintage, signifies another turning point in the trajectory of the winery yet it is an exceedingly appropriate one. That's because Terre Alte is a blend. It incorporates the heritage of different grapes. And it's the summation of input from different cultures.

In other words, we can think of Terre Alte the way we think of Friuli: as a crossroads, only of grapes instead of pathways of transportation.

Terre Alte combines Friulano, Pinot Bianco, and Sauvignon. The Pinot Bianco and Sauvignon were fermented at controlled temperatures in stainless steel tanks, while the Friulano was fermented and aged in small casks of French oak. The three wines were blended ten months later, and aged for nine months in the bottle.

With a wine of this heritage, from this particular place, you could reasonably expect a complex nose and palate and finish.

Which is, of course, what you get.

The color is medium yellow, but it's a little elusive. It catches your eye, and then tucks behind something else. On the nose you think you get yellow apple and apricot, but then lemon verbena and acacia and thyme saunter in. The palate carries some weight and viscosity, but then it finishes with a clean acidity.

This wine gets to me, maybe because Friuli gets to me.

I feel it when I stand at the low wall of the Abbey of Rosazzo, near to where Terre Alte's vineyards are located, looking out to the hills in front of me. My eyes scan the landscape, and I feel like I am *returning*. I sense that I know that curve of the road there, the rise of the hill over here, and the rush of a waterfall as an echo of what's come before.

There's no reason why I should think this. Returning to a place implies that you've been there before, but this place is not my place and this country is not my country. Not in this generation, anyway.

Some of my grandmothers were here before, maybe, their histories as elusive as my descriptors of this wine. It's an ongoing game of hide and seek. This place. This wine. Whatever I sense about them both, it's sometimes lost and mostly found.

The "cemetery" of wine in CVNE's cellars in Rioja provides the perfect environment for aging wine, and for growing mold.

Chapter Ten
How to Wander through
a Cemetery of Wine

They call it a cemetery.

Except it's a cemetery for wine.

It's a series of narrow alleyways, well below ground level, where bottles of wine are laid down to rest.

Not for all eternity, of course. Only until the winery owners decide to pull them – to sell or to sample or to share.

In the meantime, you'd be forgiven for thinking it's a little bit of a creepy place.

The below-ground alleyways contain levels of large niches on either side, each one some three or four feet square, where bottles are nestled horizontally, layer upon layer.

The texture of the niches seems like porous concrete, or maybe granite rock.

It's hard to tell. It's dimly lit, there below ground.

It's cool there, too, and damp.

Twelve degrees Celsius, in fact (about 53 degrees Fahrenheit), and 100% humidity.

They are the perfect conditions, I'm told, for mold to grow. Which is the fuzzy, stringy stuff you notice all around you, linking bottles together like fragile, spindly cables for so many pylons side by side, like a suspension bridge on a micro scale.

If there was a ghost in this cemetery, it would be made of mold.

The mold is penicillin, I'm told. And in fact it doesn't just grow, it thrives, covering the outlined walls of the niches, the exposed bottles, and even the labels that differentiate one niche from another.

It may be an omnipresent ghost, but it's a friendly one.

That's because it's an indicator, like a canary in a coal mine: the conditions are exactly what they're supposed to be here, underground, in the wine cellar of one of Rioja's best-known and most historical producers.

The mold is a function of these conditions. And it is a function of time.

Which is what you need to know about Rioja.

Time, and patience, and history.

And maybe a little about tapas.

———

North of Madrid, and south of Bilbao, is a wine region of Spain called La Rioja.

The Camino de Santiago, or Pilgrim's Route to Santiago de Compostela, passes through there.

There are ancient monasteries, and Michelin-starred restaurants, and lots and lots of tapas bars in the towns and villages of La Rioja.

The thing, as a visitor, is to pick up a packet of coupons for *pinchos*, or small tapas, and head to a street lined with tapas bars for lunch or a late dinner. Each coupon, or voucher, is valid for "un pincho estrella" and "una bebida," or a single serving of a tapa and a drink. One voucher, one serving, and no need to fuss with cash. Then you move on to the next bar and the ritual starts over again. And again. And again. (It depends which town you're in, and which street. The Calle del Laurel in Logroño, for example, boasts some 200 tapas bars.)

On one hand this part of Spain overflows with traditions the way its tapas bars overflow with customers at 10 pm on a Saturday night, or the way its religious trails and hostels overflow with tourist groups and lone seekers during the warmer months. Rioja is a place that's both ancient and reverent.

On another hand Rioja is full of young people and it's hip and bustling and envelope-pushing.

When it comes to wine, however, the traditional and the hip meet. They both slow down.

Way down.

Time is Rioja's ace up their sleeve: time spent aging, long and slow, in both bottles (remember those cemeteries…) and wooden barrels.

It is a question of patience that is both legally and temperamentally imposed. It's a shift to a whole different kind of slow, a whole different pace and flow and cadence.

The finest wines of Rioja – the Gran Reserva – are required by law to spend at least two years in oak and three additional years in bottle before their release to the market. Rioja wines labeled Crianza age for at least two years, and those labeled Reserva age for at least three years. The Gran Reserva, with the five-year minimum, age the longest of all.

They are the opposite of the immediate, drink-now approach to wine consumption so prevalent in the market today.

Rioja is wine-as-delayed-gratification.

During that time of aging, the fruit of the Tempranillo grape that most of these wines are made of will have mellowed, highlighting instead the wine's underlying balance and finesse.

They're lighter in body, but with a deep, rich color that comes from the Tempranillo. Their flavor profile is more gentle than overbearing. The edge has been taken off of many Rioja wines – the same way that the edge is taken off of foods that are cooked, or roasted, or baked. It makes for a mellow camaraderie with a wide range of dishes.

It's the distinctive aromas of Rioja wines that get me every time. They're savory -- almost peppery -- but without a sharp bite.

The aging process, for the best producers, yields wines that are somehow both friendly and profound, that are low-alcohol yet still dense with flavor. Aged Rioja wines, for me, have an extraordinary depth of character, the nuanced kind that develops with age, while still presenting an open, welcoming face to first-approachers.

I think of them the way I think of people of a certain age, non-judgmental people who relish their own position in life. They've lived long enough to form their own opinions, and the right to adjust them along the way. They've earned their own self-confidence. They know their place on the Earth. They absorb influences, and filter out the elements that enhance their own expression.

That depth of character comes, I think, from a respectful allegiance to tradition.

———

I visited the underground caves, or cemeteries, of two of Rioja's most historic and well-known producers, CVNE and R. López de Heredia Viña Tondonia.

Both wineries are located in a town called Haro. Back in the nineteenth century, several major wineries were established here, oriented around the town's railroad. Materials in. Wine out.

The storage niches of these two wineries contain bottles that were made from grapes grown at almost the same time as the railroad tracks were laid.

A hundred and thirty years ago, in CVNE's case. "The only thing that matters to me is time," says Victor Urrutia Ybarra, CVNE's CEO and the family business' fifth-generation leader. "It's the only true test, whether it's literature or architecture or wine. After time, if it isn't as good as you thought it was, then maybe it wasn't that good to begin with."

López de Heredia, by close comparison, was started by the current generation's great grandfather – Don Rafael López de Heredia y Landeta – 137 vintages ago.

When you visit, you get the sense that not a whole lot has changed, not when it comes to wine's ability to slow the passage of time.

Today Heredia's best-known wine, Viña Tondonia, takes eight years to produce.

Eight years.

That's the entire life cycle of a koala bear.

It's also how long it takes, according to Apple co-founder Steve Jobs, to do something of magnitude.

I'm pretty sure that's what Heredia was thinking with their wine.

First, the wine spends about two years in large tanks.

Then it's racked into barrels.

Then it spends six years in the barrels.

Every six months while the wine is in the barrels, Heredia staff separates the wine from the sediment that's naturally dropped to the bottom of the oak barrel. Winemaker Mercedes López de Heredia calls it "educating the wine," or taking something rough and making it softer, more elegant, and easier to drink.

Finally the wine is bottled, and it spends at least another year in bottles before it's shipped to market.

That's an exponential amount of time and resources, when you consider fermentation tanks and oak barrels and glass bottles and the storage space to put it all – multiple vintages of it all, for multiple years on end.

But Heredia makes both white and red wines the same way.

"We want to make it our way," Mercedes said. "It's really hard to make 500,000 bottles in our way."

Hard, and time-consuming. Which also means costly.

Yes, it would be more profitable for them to accelerate the maturation and stabilization processes.

Yes, it's even technically and chemically possible to do.

So why don't they? I asked.

They'd lose the quality and the typicity, they said.

The wines wouldn't develop their gentleness, they said.

We wouldn't have the time to *educate* the wines, they said.

This philosophy of slow wine carries over into many variables of the winery. The slow lifestyle decision is illustrated throughout the winery.

Here's one example.

There's a staff of coopers, which are the skilled workers who make oak barrels. The oak is imported from the U.S.' Appalachian Mountains, a source that the winery has used continually since its very beginning. The coopers engineer the barrels from the tree up, so to speak: choosing the wood, purchasing, sawing, drying and curing, toasting, assembling the barrels with their staves and hoops.

Heredia is unique in the sense that they *have* a staff of coopers, whereas most wineries simply buy the barrels already toasted and assembled. Heredia's coopers, however, also spend an inordinate amount of time repairing older barrels as well as creating new ones.

That makes sense when your barrels are used for 20 to 25 years on average, and your intention is to naturally stabilize the wine. Rather than filter their wines (which stabilizes them), Heredia relies on patience and the passage of time. Over many years and a continual process of racking or "educating" the wines from one barrel to another, the wines experience a moderate amount of oxidation without acquiring the strong woody flavors or oaky aromas that new barrels transfer.

Barrels are one example of the "slow lifestyle" seen throughout the winery. The tasting room offers a second example.

It took Heredia's winemaker eight trips to London to convince the star architect Zaha Hadid to design Heredia's tasting room. It took some convincing for the non-wine-consuming Hadid to agree to the commission. But the design — where she curves a decanter shape around the walls of the room — illustrates the winery's philosophy that, though they're dedicated and respectful of their tradition, they are far from stuck in the past.

Tasting Note: 2002 Viña Tondonia Red Reserva

The thing about drinking Viña Tondonia from López de Heredia is that you and a friend can easily empty a whole bottle before you realize what just happened.

Consider yourself forewarned.

It's a low-alcohol wine at 12.5% ABV, which helps.

But the real reason this wine has such little hit-you-over-the-head impact is that it's *fresh*.

Fresh, in terms of texture. The tannins are firm but exceptionally well-integrated, after all that time being "educated" in wood.

"You have to make the rough things softer," Mercedes López de Heredia said. "It all has to do with patience. That's what gives it the beauty of an old wine but the freshness of a young wine."

The wine will taste fresh, too, in terms of fruit – cherry especially, and berries, plus vanilla, violets, and a clean, deep earthiness.

Viña Tondonia will taste rich but almost casually rich. Understatedly rich. Comfortably rich.

It's quiet rather than showy, but with the structure and the fruit to let you know that – if you were given it in a blind tasting – *something* is up with this wine.

That something is time. The ace up Rioja's sleeve.

These pallets stacked high outside Creation Winery are as useful as they are beautiful.

Chapter Eleven
How to Build Community into Wine

I had a crazy (read "brilliant") professor in college who taught a course called the Political Geography of Africa. Here was his final exam question: "Let's say you started in Djibouti, turned south, and walked the perimeter of the entire continent of Africa. Name every country you'd pass through, in order, before you arrived back in Djibouti."

Right.

I'm sure I did not answer that question correctly. But at least I was reasonably prepared. I've always felt a pull toward Africa and fortunately my college and graduate schools encouraged that interest, through instruction in history, language, literature, culture, and geography.

At different times I had also studied abroad, in Kenya, Tanzania, and Ethiopia. But until a few years ago, even with my interest in wine, I hadn't physically set foot in South Africa, whose history in winemaking dates back to the Dutch East India Company of the seventeenth century.

I was well aware of South Africa's twentieth-century political history and turmoil, with apartheid top of mind. I was aware of its wines too, though I wasn't necessarily a fan. Somewhere along the way I had tasted one too many under-ripe Pinotage or over-oaked Chenin Blanc wines.

But then I went there on vacation, and realized that I would land midway through the answer to that final exam question, halfway around the perimeter of the continent near Cape Town and Walker Bay and Stellenbosch and some of the most visually captivating scenery I've ever had the pleasure to wander through.

This was a totally non-work related vacation, meaning I had no appointments at wineries or interviews with producers. I would see what I saw, and taste what I would.

Even so, it wasn't an easy trip. There's no escaping South Africa's history of racial divide, nor did we want to. We spent long hours at the Apartheid Museum outside Johannesburg and along Vilakazi Street in Soweto, where homes (now historical points of interest) of both Nelson Mandela and Desmond Tutu are located. These visits barely scratch the surface, obviously, of what there is to know but it was a start at creating some context for our time there.

It wasn't an easy trip, but I remember it as an encouraging one. Wine is not and never has been South Africa's most pressing concern, but it is an industry where we can see the ripple effects of a central disruption.

———

What are some of the ways that apartheid impacted South Africa's modern wine industry? And how is the wine industry emerging from that history, some 20 years on from the end of apartheid in 1994?

Apartheid handicapped – and in some ways totally stalled – South Africa's industry. The country as a whole was isolated, and its trade suffered from boycotts of South African products in protest of its apartheid system. Which meant, for example, restrictions on winemakers' access to healthy plant material for replenishing their vineyards, and it meant delayed development in terms of machinery and technology.

And, of course, apartheid meant severe inequality of employment in the vineyards and at the wineries.

This is a legacy that still reverberates, as seen in the wide racial disparity of staff and owners of wineries around the country.

Since the end of apartheid in 1994, wineries have been taking steps forward. They've been updating their viticultural and winemaking practices, reviving old-vine vineyards, and committing to sustainable agriculture – about 95% of its producers today are certified.

There have been positive steps forward socially and politically as well, as a certain kind of emotional intelligence and reflection about South Africa's divided history has emerged and begun to take hold. Solms-

Delta winery in Franschhoek, for example, was founded by Mark Astor who established a trust to benefit the estate's historically disadvantaged residents and employees. They were given equal equity stake in the winery, and some profits go toward improving residences and social programs for health and education.

In some cases, an older and more established brand is helping to create a new brand post-apartheid. Fairview Winery in Paarl, for example, gave Fairvalley Winery land to produce their own wines and they share the winemaking facility. The more established and well-known Paul Cluver brand in Elgin shares resources with the much newer Thandi brand, which is the first BEE (Black Economic Empowerment) company to win a gold medal at the International Wine Challenge.

———

Still, it isn't easy to break away from ways of thinking that were concretized and internalized over the decades of apartheid rule. It doesn't happen quickly, either.

"Here it's still a matter of survival of the fittest," said Carolyn Martin, one of the owners and founders in 2002 of Creation Wines, located in a remote corner of South Africa's Walker Bay. "At Creation we work in a cooperative way. But that is not necessarily something I learned growing up South African."

Martin attributes her approach to living abroad, in the UK and Switzerland in particular.

"When I went to the UK, I began to understand how different cultures connect and what that means," she said. "In Switzerland, I saw that communities are so successful and so wealthy because they really work together to help each other. It's less competitive, more cooperative, and they achieve greater success. That is not so usual for this area, and I'm a bit of a tall tree in that sense."

One of her greatest commitments, and excitements, is a community center project she's spearheading where 49 people — farmers and grape growers in her region – are working together for a common cause, rather than competing for a commercial advantage.

"There are lots of people in this area between Hermanus and Caledon who live really tough lives," she said. "Could you imagine that that's the pool where the next generation of brilliant people will come from?"

Martin imagines exactly that, actually. Most of her staff are local, having been born within a mountain pass or two of the winery. They were probably born during apartheid. They didn't – couldn't – travel much, and their exposure to the outside world has been limited, though it's grown in recent years. If your parents or other family members worked in the wine industry, it was as laborers in the vineyards and almost certainly not within the winery.

Yet they are exactly the pool of people that Martin seeks out and trains from the beginning. It's an unlikely set of employees, based in an even more unlikely location. And Creation Wines has achieved an unlikely success.

———

Back in 2002, Carolyn Martin considered it a miracle if one visitor a day found their way to the tasting room at Creation Wines, at the far end of a rough wilderness road that still to this day remains unpaved for more than a kilometer. Even so, the winery now welcomes more than 45,000 visitors annually.

Martin and her husband Jean-Claude were two of the company's three employees when they founded the winery. Now there are more than 30 employees plus representatives around the country.

Back in 2002, there were sheep on the land but no electricity or development in the area. Martin has turned the remoteness into an asset: today Creation Wines offers walking safaris through the vineyards as a way for visitors to appreciate the area's biodiversity.

What accounts for their growth trajectory, despite significant obstacles of geography, culture, and politics?

If you ask me, as one of those visitors who has bumped along the road to the oasis of Creation's tasting room, it's all about the buzz.

It's what you feel when you arrive, when you step into the tasting room, when you are welcomed. It's what happens when you're invited to sit and look out over this landscape. It's about the design decisions of the interior — functional, quirky, beautiful. And it's about the wine.

But if you ask Carolyn Martin what accounts for that buzz, she'll attribute it immediately to the staff. "It's so much about having the A-Team on the floor with you," she said. "They make an incredible difference in terms of their service ethic."

It's a smart move, to invest so deeply and from the ground up in the place where your business is. It's a smart move that shows business savvy, but it also shows a high level of emotional intelligence.

Emotional intelligence is the *juice*.

It's what enabled Martin to see the value of investing in local people. It's what she must have injected into their training and development. And, in turn, emotional intelligence is what enables those people to provide valuable, compassionate, truly hospitable services to guests who walk through the door.

Emotional intelligence doesn't make the wine, but it certainly helps to communicate what's great about it.

Tasting Note: 2013 Creation Wines Viognier

I first tasted this wine during a visit to Creation's tasting room, as part of their flight of wine and food pairings. The view onto the vineyards opened wide in front of us as we lounged on a sofa very much like our own sofa at home. We were *absorbing*: the buzz of this place where we'd landed, and the gift of this oasis at the end of a long road, and the surprise of what we were beginning to see was a unique and pivotal enterprise among South African wineries.

A plate of charcuterie and cheeses had already done much for our recovery from the travel, and we slowly turned to something for dessert.

"Paradoxical Wine and Chocolate Pairing" is what they call it.

It isn't that Creation is the first to offer wine and chocolate as a tasting room experience. It's that the wine and chocolate is one of many (and varied) experiences. Art exhibitions. Mini walking safaris. Secret pairings. And more. The point is that Martin and her team are experimenting, and utilizing the resources they have at hand, and not operating a business as usual.

The Viognier was the only white wine offered alongside three reds, and four chocolates were also set on the low table in front of us. Viognier, our server explained, is fairly new to vineyards in South Africa, though it's gaining quickly in popularity. Creation, not so surprisingly, was the first farm in the Hemel-en-Aarde region to plant it.

It's fuller and richer in body, without the acidity of some other white grapes like Sauvignon Blanc. Its nose is full of stone fruits like peaches and apricots, and it also expresses some floral notes like orange blossoms and acacia.

I retasted this wine back at home, many months later, in order to write this tasting note. It's ironic and cliché and also very true: wine tastes better when it's tasted in its place, when you're part of the environment and caught up in the moment.

It was true here too. There is no arguing that I had a better response to the Viognier when we were seated at the Creation winery itself, when we were feeling the buzz and joining the flow of taste that was pouring out there.

Don't get me wrong. Drinking this wine is not a hardship, no matter where you are. This time it was the nectarine that came through for me, along with a zesty lightness and spicy finish reminiscent of its Gewürztraminer cousins.

The fact that it tasted better a few months earlier is simply a testament to being in the moment, at that winery in South Africa, feeling impressed by the hospitality in what is in many ways still an inhospitable place.

This Viognier represents for me the promise of what's possible, regardless and despite and even so.

Hardy Wallace handwrote this label on his bottle of Mourvèdre. Normally he prints labels one by one while sprawled out on the living room floor of his bungalow.

Chapter Twelve
How to Be Hungry for Wine

"Be careful not to walk on the corners of the porch. You might fall through."

That advice will always be one of my first impressions of Hardy Wallace, winemaker at Dirty + Rowdy Family Wine Company in California. It was the first time I met him, a few years ago, and we were walking up to the second floor apartment of a shaky-looking bungalow north of Napa, which he shared with his fiancée Kate.

"We're afraid to walk on parts of the porch," he explained a few minutes later as we sat on the floor of their living room. "You can definitely see that the wood's all rotted, and it's slanted down. We're cool right here... I think."

That conversation, there on the floor that may or may not give way at any moment, captured for me what it means to be *hungry for wine*. Hardy Wallace may as well have been the face of the whole concept.

My desire to find others with a sense of purpose similar to Hardy's has led me around the world, and my travels have yielded exceptional narratives and refreshing discoveries. Some of them are recounted in this book.

I've noticed that, when winemakers who are hungry for wine are just starting out, they'll work two or three jobs just to keep the lights on... whatever it takes, just so they can keep making wine. If they're more established, you get the sense that they've made the slow journey to authenticity, and have somehow found peace inside the infinite challenge that is wine.

Hardy is somewhere in between – not starting out, but with lots of years of wine ahead of him yet.

Making his own wine under the Dirty + Rowdy label is his current role in the industry, but it wasn't his first. In 2009 he won Murphy-Goode Winery's "Really Goode Job" contest – there were more than 2000 entries – on the strength of his own viral marketing campaign. That job launched his wine career and served more broadly as a key moment along the trajectory of social media's influence on the wine industry: the "wine-obsessed social media and Web 2.0 expert" (which is what the job description called for) would be paid and paid well to learn about wine and generate content about it specifically for broadcast on the popular social media platforms of the time.

Hardy started out being *hungry to communicate* about wine.

———

If I had to style Hardy Wallace in a photo shoot, one of the shots would be of him in the middle of a vineyard, sitting at a desk, with a single old-fashioned black rotary-dial phone that he's looking at, waiting for it to ring, willing it to ring. That's what a lot of winemaking is, he told me once. Waiting, especially in the winter when the vines are resting. And in the meantime you're waiting for the phone to ring so that you can sell some wine and pay some bills, in order to do the whole thing all over again.

Another photo – completely the opposite in terms of tone and pace – would be of him at a large walk-around tasting, with his wrap-around eyeglasses on his nose the way an old-fashioned pilot wore them, almost goggle-like, the bottom edge close to his cheekbones, with the strap connecting one tip of an ear handle around the back of his head to the other. At a large tasting he travels at warp speed with something like warp energy and warp enthusiasm. So much to taste! So many people to talk to! So much to learn! And never enough time for any of it!

A third shot would be of him walking up the rickety stairs to that rickety porch of the bungalow that was home for him and Kate, because it dismantles so many assumptions about the photoshopped image of wine and the luxurious (if mostly fictitious) overlay of the wine lifestyle. "The only thing that I own that's surrounding me right now is this bag of corks and these cases of wine," Hardy said from the floor as he looked around him. "The couch isn't mine, we don't know whose lamp that is, and there was artwork here that someone took last week. We should get a tea kettle that whistles but man, we can use that ten dollars for something else. That's five labels. That's almost a case of glass for bottles."

Another photo would be of Hardy and Kate living in a converted old apple barn in the middle of nowhere in the foothills of the Sierra Nevada mountain range, east of Sacramento. This scenario actually happened, when they were farming a vineyard in Amador. "Our neighbor had 67 cats and serious dementia, and she ran around at four in the morning, yelling and trying to herd those cats. You put up with some weird stuff."

The value of these images, and that audio of our conversation, is that it makes wine *relatable* to everyday life. These images and those words communicate the reality of a worker, first and foremost. The hard physical labor of it, sometimes. The struggle and anxiety to make ends meet, sometimes. The frustration of it, sometimes. The patience and the occasional rewards, too.

The life of a winemaker, in other words, is anything but glamorous.

At this stage in my life, and in the life of my peers, it's the antithesis of glamour," Hardy said. "There are some people who live a very glamorous wine lifestyle. I don't think I will, ever. The work of wine is dirty work. It's hard work. You're always sticky, you're always wet, you're always cold. The glamour part has nothing to do with it. It's spending time working really hard at something that you love."

———

The end game of a life like this, for Hardy and Kate and others like them, is to make a wine that they don't even see as a drink. Instead, as Hardy says, "there's this spot at the center of the earth, and there's something that's happening there with or without us. You just happen to be a gentle participant, an observer. It's like watching birth. There's something greater than we are. You can break it down to science and yeasts, but there's something magical. Once you experience it, there's nothing else you want to do."

It's a little crazy, he admits. But, when you're that hungry for wine, it's what you do.

My friend Julius, who is a videographer, captured my interviews with several other winemakers, growers, negociants, merchants when I asked them what they think it means to be hungry for wine. Each of them naturally had their own interpretation, but the thread that links them all is the intention to almost *shepherd* their wines into being rather than to control their production.

For Jack Bittner, that approach to winemaking is also reflected in the people who ultimately buy these wines. They're curious, and often they operate a little outside standard expectations. Jack is the winemaker at Franz Hill Vineyard near Calistoga, which was originally planted in the 1870s and "resurrected" by his wife's parents after they purchased the property in 1969. The vineyard sits 1200 feet above the Napa Valley and looks out toward Mount St. Helena and the Palisades. Two small plots produce a scant 10 barrels annually, with a yield that's one-tenth the Napa average.

The people who are really hungry for wine take extra steps, he said – to understand the source and the people involved, and perhaps they even seek out styles that are not immediately gratifying or mainstream.

"The wines made *by* people who are hungry for wine, *for* people who are hungry for wine, are usually closer to the margin," he said.

Helping those "margin wines" get a broader audience is a big part of Jack's motivation. They aren't for everybody, he said. They aren't driven by a lot of fruit, and they're earthy in an Old World style. So when someone pulls the cork in Copenhagen or Vancouver or Boston, it's exciting to know that there's a connection between them and his family's tiny little patch of earth. Franz Hill is one site and the project is not scalable or even profitable; it's about preservation of a historic vineyard, and stewardship of the land, and understanding what that wine wants to be and the story it wants to tell.

Matt Licklider would have swapped in the word *authenticity* for *hungry for wine*. Licklider and Kevin O'Connor co-founded Lioco Wines in 2005 with the idea of favoring California wines with more nuance than power; they source fruit from Sonoma, Mendocino, and Santa Cruz counties.

110

"I think that's what people are hungry for, as it pertains to wine or clothing or experience," he said. "They want authenticity. So is there still a giant market for industrial grade wine? Sure. But I believe in my heart that the natural course of evolution is a movement away from that industrial experience toward something that's more authentic."

Dawnine Dyer has witnessed that evolution first-hand in California, since she began her wine career in 1974 at Mondavi. In 1976, she pioneered the use of *méthode champenoise* for sparkling wine at Domaine Chandon, which was then a Napa Valley startup. She stayed at Chandon for 24 years and is currently the winemaker at Meteor Vineyards in Napa's Coombsville area. She has also been the long-time winemaker at her and her husband's own Dyer Vineyard on Diamond Mountain.

She settled in Napa back then, she said, because it offered a peek at a lifestyle that was both rural and serene, that has the kind of risk-taking that farming has always had, and that was also very culturally engaged.

"You saw people come in and take ownership of what the qualities of wine from this place can be," she said. For Dawnine, throughout her career of more than 30 years, being hungry for wine means working with the grapes to discover what they can best achieve.

It's a more humble approach for a winemaker to step aside and let the fruit itself take center stage. It's also ironic that winemakers like these who are hungry for wine have their hunger satiated by nuance and authenticity.

They're satiated by feasting on what's subtle.

———

Hardy Wallace, Jack Bittner, Matt Licklider, and Dawnine Dyer are true examples of being hungry for wine at this moment in California. But there are many others, most of whom I'm sure I haven't even met yet.

There are many winemakers working in many regions of the world, who are hungry for different things, and for different reasons. I've tried to illustrate several of them in this book and I wanted to finish with these examples because it brings me, in a way, back full circle from where I started.

None of the people in this chapter *have* to make wine, just as I don't *have* to write about it. We choose to, for the same simple reasons I started with and explained back in this book's introduction. We choose wine because it tastes good. Because we like it. Because we want more of it in our lives. And we'll go to some fairly extraordinary lengths to get it there.

Because we are hungry.

For wine.

Tasting Note: 2011 Dirty + Rowdy Santa Barbara Highlands Mourvèdre

Sometimes a conversation shifts things around in your head. You walk away feeling bewildered or disoriented or astonished. That was true for me with Hardy Wallace. At the end of our visit he gave me this bottle of wine, and the gesture was the equivalent of a punctuation mark to that what-just-happened feeling.

The bottle had a cork but no label except for two strips of masking tape, which Hardy used as a canvas for his black Sharpie scribble: 2011 Dirty + Rowdy, Santa Barbara Highlands, Mourvèdre, with maybe his signature in the upper right-hand corner.

There's a violet tone to the color at the rim of this wine, which gradually increases to an almost-opacity at its pale ruby core. Unusual color for Mourvèdre. There are plums on the nose, and an aromatic vivacity that's fresh-picked from the savory herb section of the garden. On the palate there are soft red fruits and a gentle gaminess, but it's more fowl than boar. This wine is *juicy*, with a long, dry finish.

The first sip is intense, as you could expect from a winemaker who's humble enough to step aside and let the path from the vine to the bottle be as unobstructed as possible. It mellows as it aerates, as if the fruit breathes a sigh of relief once it's been allowed to run.

Conclusion
Just Drink the Stuff

I am in the practice of putting wine in context, which involves looking up and looking out, and seeing the many (many) hands that worked to bring a bottle of wine to the table. It is what I do, and what I enjoy.

For the last few weeks of writing this book, however, I was having a crisis.

I was feeling like I lost the simple *pleasure* of wine.

Writing so much about "context" means that I was thinking – often too much – about what was in my glass, rather than just enjoying it.

I was sure it was just a phase and it would pass. But in the meantime, one question kept nagging at me.

Could I still find simple pleasure in a glass of wine?

It was where I started. It was what I did at the very beginning. But by this point I was a long way from home.

Could I stop thinking and just drink the damn wine?

And would that be *enough*?

I had to know. So I gave it a try.

Spoiler alert: it ain't pretty.

———

There was this wine in front of me, and only this wine – two or three fingers' worth of 2004 Ontañon Bodegas Reserva from Rioja, Spain.

I picked up the glass, and right away all of my "wine training" wanted to rush back at me.

The core is opaque, with a dark cherry-colored rim.

(And are there legs? What about the saturation?)

I smell black fruits and olives.

(What kind of black fruit? What kind of olives?)

 I smell woodsy herbs, and smoke. Or ash.

(What kind of herbs? And which is it? Smoke? Or ash?)

GAH

I don't know where this is coming from, this "tasting note voice" that nudges at the parentheses of my thoughts. Yes, of course my wine teachers urged me to be specific. Yes, they encouraged me to push further with my descriptions, beyond what the others in the room were saying, beyond agreeing with the power of their suggestions.

Why did I even shift into "tasting note mode" was all I wanted to do was enjoy a few sips of wine?

That's force of habit, most likely.

But here's what wrong with that, in my opinion. I've always felt that tasting notes are like a script I should be following. There's a formula to it, like a grid. Color. Nose. Palate. Finish. Tasting notes are helpful, no doubt.

I know the rules, and I can follow them, though I sometimes feel like a dancing bear when I do.

Plus there's no section of the grid where you can indicate pleasure. There is no space for WHOOPEEEEE!!!!

All very objective, it is. Very precise.

Which is why sometimes − and for me, most times − tasting notes seem too analytical. Tasting the wine sometimes becomes over-tasting it and thinking about wine, as I can see in myself, becomes over-thinking it.

There is not much room for the *give* of circumstance.

This is the danger zone that I found myself in: over-tasting, over-thinking, defaulting into analytical notes even if they're utterly inadequate.

This is the danger zone: losing sight of the *pleasure* of wine.

I am in danger of not enjoying wine the way I started out enjoying wine -- simply for the joy of it, for the way it made me feel, because it connected me to the people I wanted to be connected to.

Losing touch with that is, indeed, GAH.

Friends I know, other wine friends, take measures against this hazard. They "take off" the whole month of January, for example, and don't drink any alcohol. At all. They're recuperating their taste buds, I think, and letting their palate rest. They're recalibrating it. But it's just as useful I think to let your brain rest too.

It reminds me of the very first teacher who taught me about wine writing, who taught me this:

Just drink the stuff.

My teacher's name was Richard, and this lesson was passed down to him as well.

He had been interviewing the Baron de Rothschild, many years ago in France, when Richard was a young man and the Baron was not. What advice would you have for me, Sir? Richard asked at the end of the conversation. What advice can you offer someone who's just starting out, who loves wine, who truly wants to know more about it, who wants to maybe even devote a good part of his life to it?

"Richard," the Baron said. "Just drink the stuff."

In other words?

Stop. Thinking.

When do I do this? When I do stop thinking, and just drink the stuff?

The answer, for me, is when I'm in the kitchen, as I'm cooking dinner.

"Could you open a bottle of wine, please?" I ask my husband.

"Of course," he says. "Anything in particular?"

"Something white," I might say, though I'm just as likely to say something red, or something sparkling, or something sweet, or something he chooses on his whim, or something that's just arrived by delivery to the front door.

And he'll go and pull something from our collection, open it, and set a half-glass full next to the chopping board as I peel carrots or dice squash or season and stuff a chicken for roasting.

He has sensed by now -- I have sensed it too -- that I am a much better cook when I have a glass of wine in my hand than when I don't.

It's kind of a joke, except it's also completely true.

I relax. I am intuitive, with seasoning the food, and with what's happening with my family as they pass and sometimes tumble through the kitchen.

These are the people -- this man, these children, often those friends – who I want to be with, as we sit at the table for dinner. These are the people I love, whose lives I want to be part of, who have a way of living that I also want to have.

The wine hasn't made this possible, exactly. But wine has helped to guide the meal to the table, and it has most likely made the food taste better, and look better, and smell better. All of that brings the people -- these people I love -- within arm's reach and encourages them to savor it and to linger, to say more and to listen longer.

This is my own hunger for wine.

This is my reason why.

At this point I don't always remember the vintage or the producer of the wine off hand.

That's actually a compliment to the wine.

Because at this point -- the best point -- wine has become a seamless layer of flavor in our lives. There's an echo of it to our conversation, and our children integrate it the way they integrate other lessons of the table, like how to make a joke or how to engage someone in conversation or how to express compassionate sympathy to a neighbor.

So.

Can I still enjoy the simple pleasure of a glass of wine?

Yes. I can.

(Most times, anyway.)

I just have to remember to do it in my kitchen, with people I love.

About the Author

Cathy Huyghe is a wine columnist at Forbes.com and Food52. Her work has also been featured in Decanter, The Atlantic, the BBC, The Boston Globe, Worth magazine, and WGBH-TV. She holds Master's degrees from the Graduate School of Design and the Journalism program at Harvard University, where she founded an organization called Harvard Alumni in Wine and Food. Cathy has worked in the kitchens of some of the world's finest chefs, including Thomas Keller, Alice Waters, and Jean-Pierre Vigato. Find her online at cathyhuyghe.com. She lives in Atlanta, Georgia with her husband, their twin boys, and their Bernese Mountain Dog.